Cambridge National

Sport Studies

There's a lot to cover for the Cambridge National in Sport Studies, but don't worry — help is at hand from the revision experts!

This brilliant CGP Revision Guide is full of clear and concise explanations for every unit of the course. There are also plenty of top tips and advice for the exam and assignments, all in CGP's classic style. It's a winner!

Unlock your Online Edition

Just scan the QR code below or go to cgpbooks.co.uk/extras and enter this code!

1583 3996 5421 9459

By the way, this code only works for one person. If somebody else has used this book before you, they might have already claimed the code.

Revision Guide

Contents

Getting Started
Course Overview 2

Unit R184 — Contemporary Issues in Sport

Topic Area 1: Issues Affecting Participation
User Groups 3
Barriers to Participation 5
Overcoming Barriers 8
Popularity of Sport 10
Emerging and New Sports 13

Topic Area 2: Promoting Values
Sporting Values 14
Olympic and Paralympic Values 16
Sporting Initiatives 18
Sporting Behaviour 20
Performance Enhancing Drugs 22

Topic Area 3: Hosting Major Sporting Events
Types of Sporting Events 24
Hosting Sporting Events — Pre-Event 25
Hosting Sporting Events 27
Hosting Sporting Events — Post-Event 30

Topic Area 4: National Governing Bodies
National Governing Bodies 32

Topic Area 5: Technology in Sport
Technology in Sport 35
Positive Effects of Technology in Sport 38
Negative Effects of Technology in Sport 39

Unit R185 — Performance and Leadership in Sports Activities

Topic Area 1: Components of Performance
Components of Performance 40
Managing Performance 42

Topic Area 2: Improving Performance
Identifying Strengths and Weaknesses 43
Improving Performance 44
Measuring Improvement 46

Topic Area 3: Planning Sports Activities
Planning Sports Activities 47
Planning Sports Activities Safely 49
Planning Activities to Meet Objectives 50

Topic Area 4: Leading Sports Activities
Organising Sports Activities 52
Leading Sports Activities 53

Topic Area 5: Reviewing Activity Planning
Reviewing Activity Planning 56
Planning Improvements 57

Unit R186 — Sport and the Media

Topic Area 1: Sporting Media Sources
Sport and the Media 58

Topic Area 2: Positive Effects of the Media in Sport
Positive Effects of the Media in Sport 61

Topic Area 3: Negative Effects of the Media in Sport
Negative Effects of the Media in Sport 64

Unit R187 — Increasing Awareness of Outdoor and Adventurous Activities

Topic Area 1: Provision of Outdoor Activities
Provision of Outdoor Activities 67

Topic Area 2: Equipment, Clothing and Safety
Equipment, Clothing and Technology 70
Types of Terrain and Environment 71

Topic Area 3: Planning Outdoor Activities
Planning Outdoor Activities 72

Topic Area 4: Evaluating Outdoor Activities
Evaluating Outdoor Activities 74

About the Exam 75
Index 77

Published by CGP

Editors: Helen Clements, Liam Dyer, Sharon Keeley-Holden, Alison Palin, Adam Worster

Reviewers: Chris Cope, Sheryl Gale, Catherine Ruth

With thanks to Robbie Driscoll for the proofreading.

With thanks to Laura Jakubowski for the copyright research.

Topic area wording on page 2 reproduced with permission of OCR.

Graph of participation rates in sports on page 10 based on data from 2015-2021 © Sport England.

The Olympic Creed and Olympic Rings logo on page 16 used with permission of the International Olympic Committee.

YouTube TV™ service is a trademark of Google LLC and this book is not endorsed or affiliated with Google in any way.

ISBN: 978 1 83774 058 1
Printed by Elanders Ltd, Newcastle upon Tyne.
Graphics from Corel® and Getty PA

Text, design, layout and original illustrations © Coordination Group Publications Ltd. (CGP) 2023
All rights reserved.

Based on the classic CGP style created by Richard Parsons.

Photocopying more than one section of this book is not permitted, even if you have a CLA licence.
Extra copies are available from CGP with next day delivery • 0800 1712 712 • www.cgpbooks.co.uk

Getting Started

Course Overview

Here's the scoop on what your Cambridge National in Sport Studies course will involve...

There are Two Mandatory Units and One Optional Unit

Unit R184 — Contemporary Issues in Sport

Unit R184 is mandatory.
It's divided into five topic areas:
1) Issues which affect participation in sport
2) The role of sport in promoting values
3) The implications of hosting a major sporting event for a city or country
4) The role National Governing Bodies play in the development of their sport
5) The use of technology in sport

For this unit, you'll sit an exam that lasts 1 hour and 15 minutes.

R184 is worth 40% of your total grade.

See page 75 for more on the exam.

Unit R185 — Performance and Leadership in Sports Activities

Unit R185 is mandatory.
It's divided into five topic areas:
1) Key components of performance
2) Applying practice methods to support improvement in a sporting activity
3) Organising and planning a sports activity session
4) Leading a sports activity session
5) Reviewing your own performance in planning and leading a sports activity session

R185 is worth 40% of your total grade.

You will choose two activities from an approved list.
They can be individual sports, team sports, or one of each.

Your teacher will give you an assignment to complete. It will have five tasks.

Task	1	2	3	4	5
Marks	28	14	14	14	10

Unit R186 — Sport and the Media

Unit R186 is optional.
It's divided into three topic areas:
1) The different sources of media that cover sport
2) Positive effects of the media in sport
3) Negative effects of the media in sport

Your teacher will give you an assignment to complete. It will have three tasks.

Task	1	2	3
Marks	12	16	12

You will either study R186 or R187 — they are worth 20% of your total grade.

Unit R187 — Increasing Awareness of Outdoor and Adventurous Activities

Unit R187 is optional.
It's divided into four topic areas:
1) Provision for different types of outdoor and adventurous activities in the UK
2) Equipment, clothing and safety aspects of participating in outdoor and adventurous activities
3) Plan for and be able to participate in an outdoor and adventurous activity
4) Evaluate participation in an outdoor and adventurous activity

Your teacher will give you an assignment to complete. It will have four tasks.

Task	1	2	3	4
Marks	6	12	12	10

Getting Started

Unit R184 — Topic Area 1: Issues Affecting Participation

User Groups

First up, you need to know about the different types of participant in sport and their needs.

Different User Groups Participate in Sport

1) People can be placed into a user group, based on things they have in common with others, such as their age or whether they work.
2) People will belong to more than one user group.
3) You need to know each of the twelve user groups below.

Some sports, e.g. korfball or quadball, are played with mixed-gender teams.

People of different genders

1) Different genders have different opportunities in sport, e.g. traditionally most sports are split into men's and women's categories.
2) There is much debate over gender in sport, particularly with regards to transgender and non-binary athletes.

People from different ethnic groups

An ethnic group shares a common cultural background — this could include the same race, language or religion.

Young children

Children from birth to the end of primary school, e.g. 0-11 years old.

Teenagers / adolescents

Children in compulsory secondary education, e.g. 11-18 years old.

Retired people / over 60s

Retired people no longer work and may receive money from a pension. Most people retire in their 60s.

Parents (singles or couples)

A single person or couple raising children.

Carers

Adults or children who care for family members, e.g. a parent or relative with a disability.

Families with children

Families are the parents or carers together with the children they are raising.

People with family commitments

People who need to spend regular time with family members.

People who work

People who have a job (in employment).

Unemployed / economically disadvantaged people

Unemployed people have no job, which can cause them to be economically disadvantaged (have a lack of disposable income). Employed people can also be economically disadvantaged if their job is low-paid or they have other financial commitments.

Disposable income is the money available after essentials (e.g. bills and food) are paid for.

People with disabilities

People with a physical or mental impairment, which may affect their ability to carry out day-to-day activities.

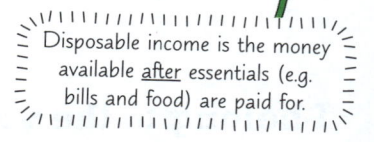

Unit R184 — Topic Area 1: Issues Affecting Participation

User Groups

User Groups have Different Needs for Sport

1) All user groups benefit from regular exercise.
2) Different sports and physical activities may appeal to different user groups.
3) Each user group also has specific needs when participating in sport.
4) These include things such as the type of exercise, cost and time available.
5) Here are some examples:

> **Young children** — this user group will need activities that are fun and engaging and take place before or after school hours.

> **Retired people** — this user group will be likely to need exercises that are less intense and low impact, as older people often have more mobility issues and health conditions.

> **Economically disadvantaged people** — this user group will need activities that are local (as they may lack transport) and are affordable or subsidised.

> **People from different ethnic groups** — e.g. people from certain ethnic groups may need private changing rooms in sports facilities (see p.8) because of religious reasons.

Sports can be Adapted for Disabilities

1) There are a wide range of disabilities, including visual, hearing, physical and intellectual disabilities. Many disabilities are non-visible (a condition that is not obvious).
2) Some disabilities don't prevent people participating in sport or physical activity alongside non-disabled participants.
3) However, some sports have been adapted, or created, so that they're more accessible, e.g.:

> **goalball** — a team sport for people with visual impairments, where the aim is to throw a ball with bells inside towards their opponents' goal.

All participants wear eye coverings, so fully-sighted and visually-impaired people can play goalball together.

> **boccia** — a team or individual sport for people with physical impairments, where players throw, kick or roll leather balls towards a white target ball.

4) It's also important that all user groups have the same access to facilities and information. For example, specialist equipment or systems can help those with disabilities and the elderly:

> - Pool hoists — chairs that help lower disabled swimmers into the water.
> - Braille — a system of raised dots on leaflets and signs that assists visually impaired people.
> - Hearing (induction) loops — a sound system that assists wearers of hearing aids.

I belong to the young, cool and attractive user groups...

There are many different user groups to learn and some have quite similar needs. The important thing to remember is that all people will belong to more than one user group, depending on their circumstances.

Unit R184 — Topic Area 1: Issues Affecting Participation

Barriers to Participation

Many different factors can prevent someone from participating in sport or physical activity.

Barriers Get in the Way of Participating in Sport

1) A barrier is something that stops people from participating in regular sport and physical activity.
2) There are many barriers that people may have to overcome to participate.
3) Each barrier affects certain user groups more than others — the tables on the next three pages give examples of these barriers and the different user groups they are most likely to apply to.

There are Barriers to Accessing Sporting Activities

Lack of transport

People need to travel to sports facilities — this could include cycling, driving or using public transport.

User Group	Barrier
Young children	Children are too young to drive or use public transport alone, so will rely on parents or carers to get them to facilities.
Retired people / over 60s	Older people may be less likely to drive and more reliant on public transport, but there may be a lack of buses or trains in their local area.
People with disabilities	Not all public transport is accessible to those with physical impairments, e.g. some train stations have no ramp access.

Lack of awareness of provision

Some people may be unaware of the opportunities they have to get involved in sport.

User Group	Barrier
People from different ethnic groups	Some people immigrating to the UK may only speak English as a second language. They won't know which activities are available in their local area and may find it more difficult to find this information.
Teenagers	Teenagers may be unaware of activities if the adverts are targeting the wrong audience — e.g. teenagers may be unlikely to see an advert in a newspaper, but more likely to see an advert on social media.
People with disabilities	People with visual impairments may not know what sports are available if information is not provided in an accessible format, e.g. leaflets in Braille.

Lack of activity provision

Insufficient equipment or facilities and unappealing activities can be a barrier to many user groups.

User Group	Barrier
People of different genders	Some facilities may only offer an activity for a single gender, e.g. they may have a rugby team for men only.
Young children	Schools may provide a limited range of activities, which some children may not enjoy.
People with disabilities	Facilities may not provide specialist equipment, e.g. pool hoists or ramps for wheelchair users.

Unit R184 — Topic Area 1: Issues Affecting Participation

Barriers to Participation

These Barriers are to do with Cost and Time

Lack of disposable income

There are various costs involved in sport, such as travelling to facilities and buying necessary clothing and equipment. Some sports are very expensive, such as skiing or equestrian (horse riding).

User Group	Barrier
Unemployed / economically disadvantaged people	This group has little money left after buying essentials, so may be unable to spend money on sport.
Young children	Children do not earn any money, so must rely on their parents or carers to pay for sports that they want to take part in.
Parents / families with children	Raising children is expensive, so families with children may have limited money to spend on sport.

Employment and unemployment

Being in or out of work can also be a barrier to participation in sport.

User Group	Barrier
People who work	Working people can only take part in sport or physical activity outside of their working hours. If they work shifts or irregular hours, it can be hard to join clubs that meet in the evening or on the weekend.
Unemployed / economically disadvantaged people	These people may spend lots of time looking for work or may work multiple low-paid jobs, so have no free time to take part in sport.

Family commitments

People from many user groups have to look after family members, which can be very difficult, especially for single parents who do not have a partner to help them.

User Group	Barrier
Parents / families with children	Parents may not have the time and energy for physical activity whilst taking care of their baby or young child. Single parents may struggle to exercise without arranging for a babysitter or using a crèche (childcare facility).
Carers	Carers may not be able to leave the person they care for unattended, which means they can't take part in sport.

Unit R184 — Topic Area 1: Issues Affecting Participation

Barriers to Participation

Other Barriers Include a Lack of Role Models or Biased Media Coverage

Lack of positive sporting role models

A role model is someone inspirational who you look up to. A lack of sporting role models within a user group will not motivate members of that group to try the sport.

It's called fashion darling.

User Group	Barrier
People of different genders	Women have lower participation rates in sport than men, so women often have fewer sporting role models to choose from.
Retired people / over 60s	Many professional sportspeople will have retired from competing before they are 60, so aren't suitable role models for older people.
People with disabilities	Disabled and adapted sports have low media coverage, so there are few disabled athletes who can act as sporting role models.

Lack of positive family role models / family support

Parents and carers can influence the physical activity of their child. The habits that are formed as a child will likely carry over into adulthood.

User Group	Barrier
Young children	Children may not take part in sport if their parent or carer isn't very active or has a negative attitude towards sport.
Teenagers	Teenagers likely won't have money or transport, so can't take part in physical activity without support from a parent or carer.

Lack of equal media coverage

The media includes TV, radio and newspapers. They promote some sports more than others. Sometimes they describe stereotypes of a user group — these are simplified ideas of a whole user group that aren't always true.

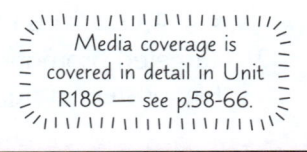

Media coverage is covered in detail in Unit R186 — see p.58-66.

User Group	Barrier
People of different genders	1) There is an imbalance of media coverage of men's and women's sports, e.g. there is greater TV coverage of men's football than women's football. 2) There are also outdated attitudes in the media that label some sports as being for 'men' or 'women' only, which can put people off participating.
People from different ethnic groups	1) There is a lack of media coverage of sportspeople from ethnic minorities, and sometimes discrimination and racism towards these groups. 2) Images used to promote sports may reinforce stereotypes, e.g. black athletes used for speed events and white athletes for sports such as golf. 3) Sporting pundits (experts who analyse sporting events and give opinions) may also not come from a diverse range of ethnic groups.

Step 1: Role Model. Step 2: Run down the hill and collect it...

There are other barriers that are more general and can affect all user groups, such as lack of confidence or low fitness. In the exam, you should always give barriers that are specific to the user group in the question.

Unit R184 — Topic Area 1: Issues Affecting Participation

Overcoming Barriers

Now for a few pages on some of the solutions that help people overcome the barriers to participation.

Facilities Should Provide a Wide Range of Sessions

Facilities are purpose-built areas where physical activity takes place, e.g. leisure centres or swimming pools.

Provision of programmes, sessions and activities

People who provide sessions at facilities should take steps to meet each user group's needs:
1) Introduce a wide range of activities to make sure there is something for everyone.
2) Include activities that all members of a family can join in with, e.g. 'parent and child' sessions, to help develop a positive relationship with sport from an early age.
3) Have classes that can be done in the home, e.g. online exercise classes.
4) Respect different cultural norms, e.g. offer women-only sessions, for women who only take part in single-sex sport due to religious beliefs.

Times for different user groups

1) Facilities can also extend opening hours so they open earlier or close later in the day.
2) This allows people who work full time or have family commitments more opportunity to access them.

Some gyms are open 24 hours a day.

Promotion Strategies Increase Participation

Promotion strategies are used to inform people about available activities and persuade them to take part.

Targeted promotions

1) Targeted promotions are special offers for a specific user group, e.g. a TV advert promoting 50% off a fitness class for elderly adults only.
2) Targeted promotions are advertised where the user group will most likely see it. E.g. posters in nurseries for parents and adverts on social media for teenagers.

Other strategies include offering taster sessions — see next page.

Role models

1) Some groups, e.g. women or people with disabilities, have fewer sporting role models.
2) Promoting role models from these groups increases participation:
   E.g. promoting the success of Hannah Cockroft, who has 7 Paralympic gold medals in wheelchair racing events (as of 2022), can inspire other people with disabilities to participate in sport.
3) Facilities can hire more diverse coaches to attract a more diverse community.
4) There should also be inclusion of ethnically diverse male and female pundits at sporting events.

Sporting initiatives

1) Sporting initiatives are campaigns that promote physical activity and get people involved in sport.
2) Examples include THIS GIRL CAN and Chance to Shine.

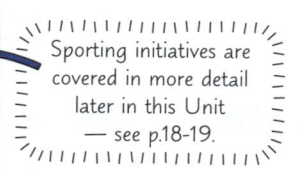

Sporting initiatives are covered in more detail later in this Unit — see p.18-19.

Unit R184 — Topic Area 1: Issues Affecting Participation

Overcoming Barriers

Improving Access is Important Too

Transport availability

1) Better and cheaper transport links make it easier for people to get to sports facilities.
2) Some people, such as those of state pension age and people with certain disabilities, are entitled to free off-peak bus travel.
3) Many urban areas have cycle lanes. Hiring a bike can be a more affordable, efficient and healthy way to access facilities in these areas.

Adapting facilities

1) Facilities can provide equipment for use by specific user groups, e.g. low-impact machines such as cross trainers for over 60s.
2) Facilities should have specialist equipment to help people with disabilities (see p.4), and introduce signs and leaflets in a variety of languages to help certain ethnic minorities.
3) Crèche facilities can be provided to care for children, so that parents can participate in physical activity, e.g. attend a yoga class.

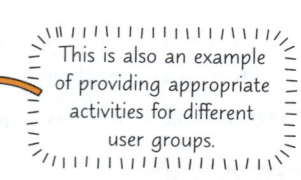

This is also an example of providing appropriate activities for different user groups.

Making Sport Cheaper is Another Solution

Concessions

Concessions are reduced prices — clubs can offer concessions for classes or membership for user groups such as retired adults or people who are unemployed who have less money to spend on sport.

Taster sessions

Free sessions encourage people to try their local facilities. They can experience a sport or class before they have to pay anything ('try before they buy').

Free parking

Leisure centres often offer free parking, which reduces the overall cost of participating in classes.

Hiring equipment

Equipment can be expensive, so facilities may allow people to hire equipment for free or at a reasonable cost. This is useful for trying a new sport because you can hire equipment first and buy your own later.

Hurdlers have to overcome all sorts of barriers...

Loads of solutions to overcoming barriers to participation were thrown at you there. Think about your own experiences and barriers you have faced, and which solutions could have helped overcome those barriers.

Unit R184 — Topic Area 1: Issues Affecting Participation

Popularity of Sport

There are many factors that can positively and negatively affect the popularity of sports in the UK.

Data can Show Popular Sports and Trends

1) Some sports in the UK are much more popular than others:

   - Football is widely watched and played because it has high media coverage and there are football pitches in all areas of the country.
   - Skiing is less popular because it has low media coverage and requires expensive equipment and access to mountainous areas or purpose-built facilities.

2) Data can be collected and analysed to see which sports and physical activities are most popular and whether there are any trends in participation (increases or decreases over time).

3) Take a look at this example from the Sport England Active Lives survey.

EXAMPLE

People aged 16 and over in the UK were asked if they had participated in different sports categories at least twice in the last 28 days. The graph shows the results.

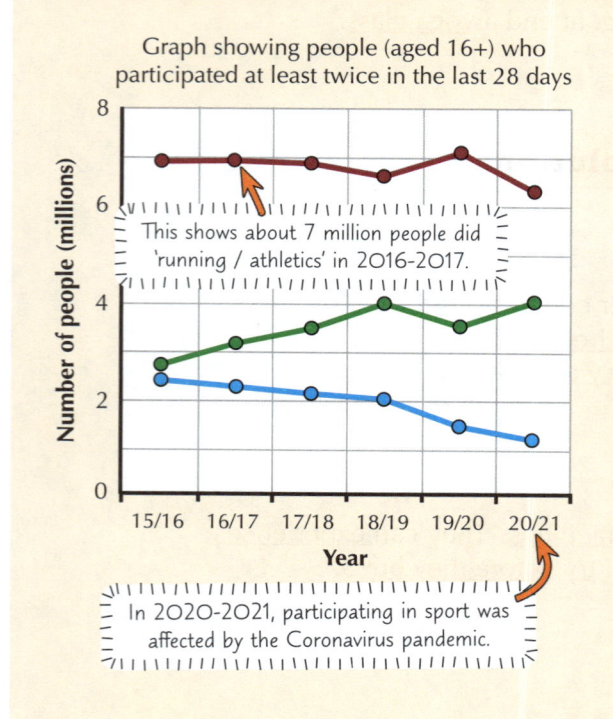

Graph showing people (aged 16+) who participated at least twice in the last 28 days

This shows about 7 million people did 'running / athletics' in 2016-2017.

In 2020-2021, participating in sport was affected by the Coronavirus pandemic.

- **Running / athletics**: e.g. running, jogging or track and field events.
- **Adventure / water sports**: e.g. hiking, high ropes and canoeing.
- **Racket sports**: e.g. tennis, badminton and squash.

The graph shows:
- Running / athletics was a more popular activity than both racket sports and adventure / water sports in all years.
- Participation in adventure / water sports increased between 2015 and 2021 (from about 2.7 to 4 million people).
- Participation in racket sports decreased between 2015 and 2021 (from about 2.4 to 1.2 million people).

Popularity Increases if There are Lots of Participants

1) If there are lots of participants in a sport or event, then more people are likely to know about it, and its popularity increases.
2) For example, around the time the London Marathon takes place, more people will take up running (the popularity of running increases).
3) Likewise, if there is a decrease in the number of participants in a sport or event, then fewer people will be aware of it, and its popularity decreases further.

Unit R184 — Topic Area 1: Issues Affecting Participation

Popularity of Sport

Popularity Depends on Provision of Facilities

1) You need access to facilities (e.g. swimming pools, tennis courts) to participate in certain sports.
2) The level of provision varies in the UK, but you'll have greater access to facilities in a city than a rural area.
3) There are many public leisure centres and volunteer-run sessions which are open to everyone. Private clubs are more expensive to join, but often include more modern equipment.
4) Some facilities are very common, such as 4G pitches. Team sports (e.g. football) that use these pitches are accessible and therefore popular.
5) Some sports require specialist facilities, like ice rinks and velodromes (a cycling arena). You are unlikely to take part in these sports regularly if you live in an area without these facilities.

Environmental Factors and Weather Affect Choice

1) Where you live affects the types of sport that are available to you.

- The UK has lots of coastline and many rivers and lakes, so water sports like sailing are more accessible than in many other countries.
- There are few snowy mountain ranges in the UK, so most people can only take part in snow sports, such as skiing, on artificial ski slopes.

2) The weather also has an effect on the popularity of outdoor sports.
3) The UK gets a lot of rain, which can delay some sporting events, such as Test cricket matches. This can be annoying for spectators, who may lose interest in a sport that is always interrupted.
4) However, many team sports can be played on all-weather pitches, e.g. MUGAs (multi-use games areas) and 4G pitches. These sports can be played in poor weather as the pitches don't freeze or flood.

Watching Live Sport can Increase Interest

1) Sport can be watched live in person or on TV.
2) Watching a sport can encourage people to participate in it themselves — so if there are lots of opportunities to watch it, its popularity will increase.
3) E.g. watching the Tour de France (a cycling event) may encourage someone to take up cycling.
4) However, if there are few opportunities to view a live sport, fewer people will participate. Limited opportunities to watch sport are due to a lack of facilities or low media coverage (see below).

Catch-up programmes allow people to watch sporting events at times that suit them.

Sports have a Range of Media Coverage

1) The media (e.g. TV, radio and newspapers) can increase awareness of a sport.
2) Some sports, e.g. football, receive lots of media coverage, which helps to maintain their popularity.
3) Other sports are rarely shown in the media, e.g. table tennis and skiing.
4) TV is the most accessible way to watch live sport. The BBC televises many sporting events, such as Wimbledon (a tennis tournament). Many people can access BBC channels on a TV, so a wider audience can watch these events.
5) However, other sporting events are shown on subscription channels, such as Sky Sports or TNT Sports (originally BT Sport).
6) There is more cost involved to access these channels, which can be a barrier for some user groups.

See p.58-66 for more on sport and the media.

Unit R184 — Topic Area 1: Issues Affecting Participation

Technology in Sport

Technology can Help Officials Make Correct Decisions

Many sports now make use of officiating technology during matches to help referees and umpires. These systems aim to make the sport fairer and take some responsibility away from on-field officials.

Hawk-Eye (tennis)

Hawk-Eye uses optical tracking technology to track the path and spin of balls, as well as the athlete's skeleton during play in multiple sports. In tennis, it's used so that performers can challenge decisions about whether shots are in or out.

Decision Review System (DRS) (cricket)

Performers are allowed to challenge an umpire's decision and have it reviewed by the third umpire, who uses various bits of technology (including Hawk-Eye) to decide whether the on-field umpire was correct or not.

'Owzaaaat?!

Television Match Official (TMO) (rugby union)

The TMO is an extra official who watches video replays. The referee on the pitch can consult with the TMO to help them make key decisions.

Video Assistant Referee (VAR) (football)

The VAR watches the match on various screens and can watch slow-motion replays. They advise the on-field referee of any 'clear and obvious' errors they have made which resulted in a goal or a player being sent off (red card).

Technology has Changed the Experience for Spectators

Technology has affected how spectators can interact with a live sporting event. Here are some ways the experience has changed for spectators:

- Commentators and pundits explain key decisions, strategies and tactics during a sporting event, which can help new spectators to understand what is going on.
- Different camera angles are used to give a chance to see something happen from many different perspectives, e.g. a goal in football.
- Sometimes performers wear cameras, e.g. a batter in cricket, to show spectators what the sport looks like from their perspective — spectators can feel more part of the action.
- Modern stadiums have big screens, which show replays to spectators. This helps to keep spectators engaged, even if they miss what happened in the moment.
- Broadcast media, including TV subscription channels, e.g. Sky Sports, has made it easier for people to watch sport from their homes and on smartphones.
- Social media allows spectators to more easily express their opinions of a sporting event and the performances of their favourite teams or players.

Unit R186 also covers how TV and social media affect sport.

I could be a TMO — they just sit around watching sport on TV...

The advancements in technology mean that sport has become accessible to spectators almost anywhere in the world. This has helped some sports become even more popular than they were before, e.g. football.

Unit R184 — Topic Area 5: Technology in Sport

Positive Effects of Technology in Sport

There are many positive effects of technology in sport for both performers and spectators. This page recaps all of the key information about technology from p.35-37.

Technology can Affect Performers in a Positive Way

Technology has many positive effects for the performers:

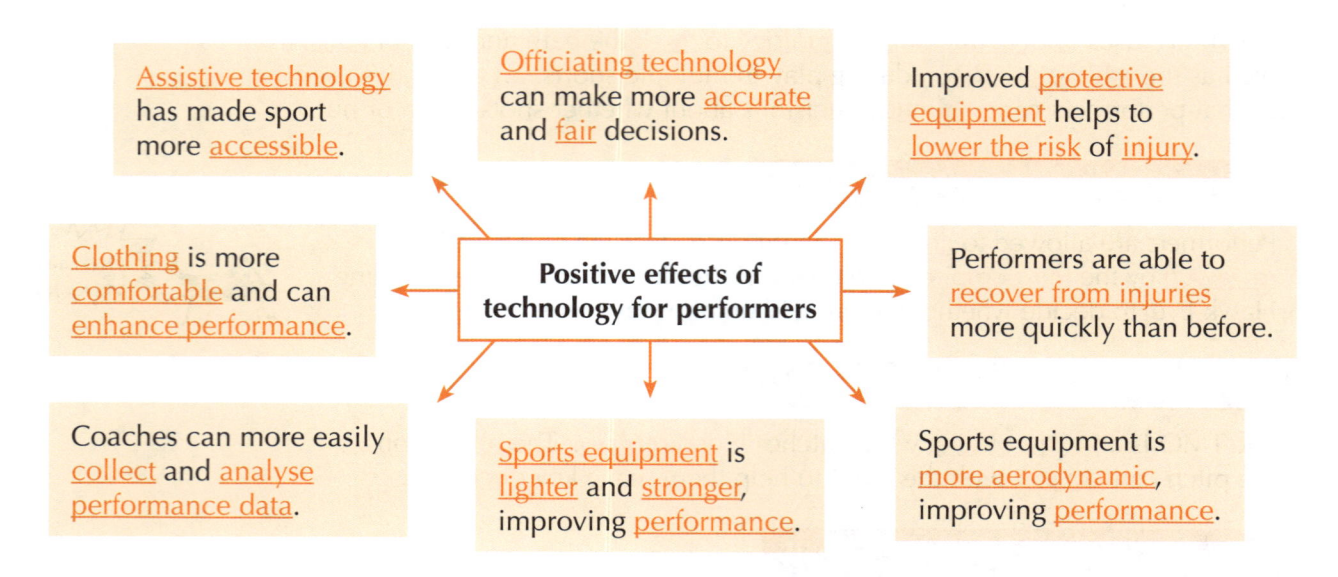

Positive effects of technology for performers

- Assistive technology has made sport more accessible.
- Officiating technology can make more accurate and fair decisions.
- Improved protective equipment helps to lower the risk of injury.
- Clothing is more comfortable and can enhance performance.
- Performers are able to recover from injuries more quickly than before.
- Coaches can more easily collect and analyse performance data.
- Sports equipment is lighter and stronger, improving performance.
- Sports equipment is more aerodynamic, improving performance.

Spectators can be Positively Affected by Technology

Technology has many positive effects for the spectators:

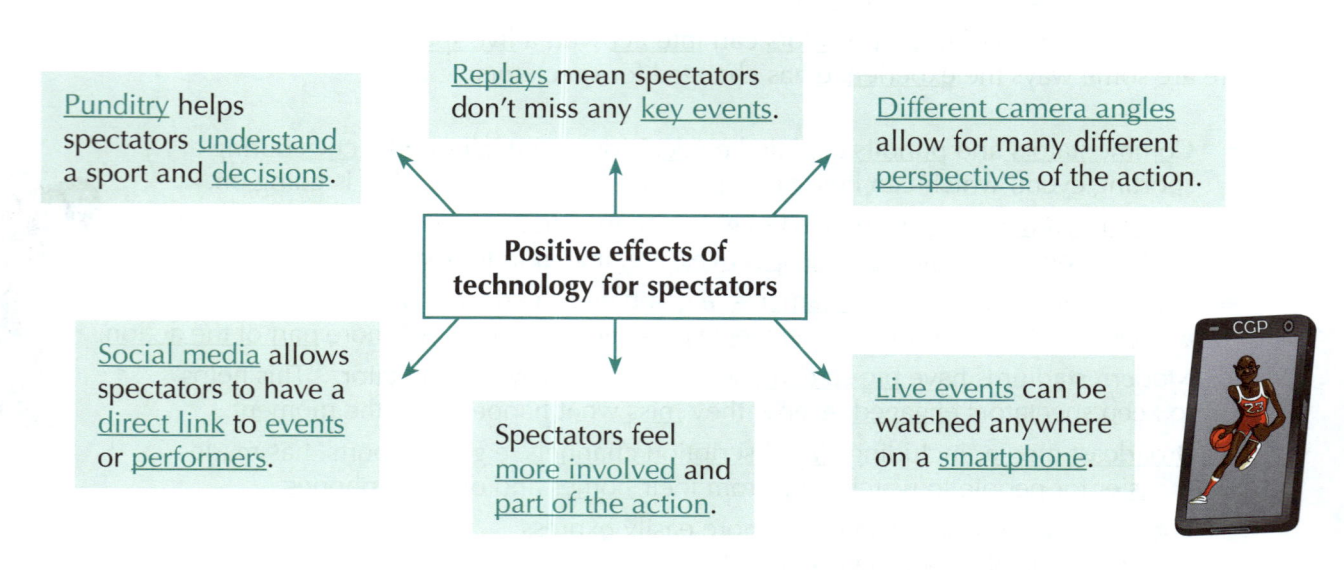

Positive effects of technology for spectators

- Punditry helps spectators understand a sport and decisions.
- Replays mean spectators don't miss any key events.
- Different camera angles allow for many different perspectives of the action.
- Social media allows spectators to have a direct link to events or performers.
- Spectators feel more involved and part of the action.
- Live events can be watched anywhere on a smartphone.

I'll have another joke ready for you in just a few moments...

Technology has really changed the way sports are played. Take a look at some videos of your favourite sport from the 1960s and compare it to how your chosen sport is played today. Make notes of all the differences.

Unit R184 — Topic Area 5: Technology in Sport

Negative Effects of Technology in Sport

Technology can be useful, but it does have limitations and negative effects for performers and spectators too.

Technology can Affect Performers in a Negative Way

Unequal access to technology

- Participants can have an unfair advantage if they have greater access to technology than their competitors. E.g. a sprinter with the latest pair of spiked shoes will have an advantage over someone wearing regular trainers.
- People are prevented from accessing the same quality of technology because of cost or their location (see below).

Gah, I thought these spikes would help!

Cost and availability of technology

- Technology is expensive, which means it is more common in wealthy countries that can afford it.
- For example, richer countries (like the UK) can build better-performing track bicycles than other countries, which gives them a significant advantage in international events.
- Even within a country, only private clubs or professional sports teams are likely to have the money to afford or invest in the newest technology.

Interrupting a game

- Officiating technology can interrupt the flow of a game and the momentum of a team or performer. For example, a rugby game comes to a complete stop while the TMO (see p.37) makes a decision.
- In some sports, e.g. cricket, officiating technology is used on request. This means it can be misused to waste time and interrupt the flow of the other team.

Influencing decisions

- Officiating technology can sometimes influence a decision in a way that doesn't use the best interpretation of the rules.
- For example, the VAR (see p.37) could decide a footballer's shoulder was in an offside position. Some people argue that it's not in the spirit of the game to disallow goals for such fine margins.

Spectators can be Negatively Affected by Technology

- Constant breaks in a game for officiating technology can be frustrating for spectators. It can reduce excitement for fans because they can't celebrate a goal or wicket if the decision could be overturned by technology.
- Replays shown on big screens in stadiums and on TVs may cause spectators to question the decisions of officials.
- Spectators have easy access to statistics, which may lead to criticism aimed at performers who aren't performing well.
- Some spectators can't afford to pay for a TV subscription channel that shows the sport they want to follow.

Why can't sharks play football? There's no one to of-fish-iate...

Some people argue that using technology in sport isn't necessarily a good thing. Think about your favourite sport and list the pros and cons of using technology for that sport (consider the performers and spectators).

Unit R184 — Topic Area 5: Technology in Sport

Components of Performance

In the assessment for this unit, you will perform in two activities, chosen from an approved activity list (found on the OCR website) — you can do two team sports, two individual sports or one of each.

There are Individual and Team Sports

Some sports are played individually or in teams, e.g. singles and doubles tennis.

Individual sports

In an individual sport, a participant competes by themselves against at least one opponent. Examples include boxing, golf, swimming, diving and skiing.

Team sports

In a team sport, a group of players compete together against an opposing team. Examples include volleyball, water polo, cricket, ice hockey and rugby.

Each Sport Needs a Combination of Different Skills

1) Skills are learned talents or abilities needed to perform a sport.
2) The level of a performer's skills will affect how well they're able to perform.

Basic and Complex Skills

- Basic skills are 'simple' skills that are used in many different sports. These include running, throwing, catching or jumping.
- Complex skills are more difficult as they combine basic skills together. These skills are specific to each sport, e.g. bowling in cricket.

3) A technique is how you carry out a skill — using a good technique means you'll be able to perform a skill well.
4) Some performers may use a different technique for the same skill. E.g. two table tennis players may generate spin in different ways when performing a forehand serve.

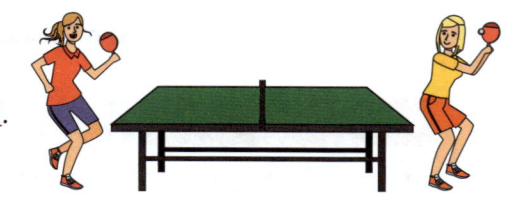

Performers Use Strategies and Tactics to Beat Opponents

Strategies and tactics are plans that improve the chance of a performer or team winning.

Strategy

Definition: A long-term plan for how to achieve an aim, e.g. winning a tournament.

Strategies are thought of before competition — it is hard to adapt a strategy quickly.
- A cyclist may decide to break away from the pack after any difficult climbs.
- A rugby team may play defensively and aim to counter-attack their opposition.

Tactics

Definition: A short-term plan for a specific situation, e.g. how to beat a particular opponent.

Tactics are adapted during competition, often based on an opponent's weaknesses.
- A boxer may be more aggressive with their punches if an opponent looks tired.
- A tennis player may use drop shots against an opponent playing from the baseline (far from the net).

Components of Performance

Compositional Ideas are Important in Artistic Sports

1) Composition is creating and arranging something, e.g. a sequence of movements.
2) Performers often express themselves using changes in speed and style.
3) Composition is important for many artistic sports, e.g. gymnastics or figure skating, where routines are judged based on things such as difficulty and execution.
4) Composition can also be used in team sports, e.g. corner and free kick routines in football.

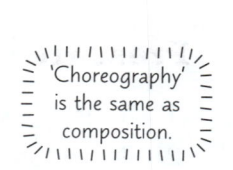

'Choreography' is the same as composition.

Creativity can Give You an Advantage

1) Creativity in sport is the ability to solve a problem in a unique way.
2) This often involves performing a skill or technique that an opponent doesn't expect.
3) A creative use of skills will not always succeed, but if they work they can outsmart an opponent and give you a competitive advantage.

EXAMPLES

Individual sports:
- A dancer may communicate a theme to an audience in a creative performance.
- A rock climber may climb a different route compared to other performers.
- A badminton player may use a flick serve to surprise an opponent who is close to the net.

EXAMPLES

Team sports:
- A basketball player may feint (pretend to throw or dribble), then quickly move off in another direction.
- A bowler in cricket may repeat the same delivery many times, then change the speed or spin of the next ball.
- A footballer may try to 'nutmeg' a defender (kick the ball through the legs).

Decision-Making is Making the Right Choice at the Right Time

1) Decision-making involves making choices based on external factors, such as the position of your opponents or teammates.
2) Performers often need good reaction times to make decisions quickly during competition.
3) A skilled performer will have more options and know the most appropriate action to take.

EXAMPLES

Individual sports:
- A golfer must select the correct shot based on the distance to the hole, hazards (e.g. bunkers) and the wind.
- A trampolinist must adjust their position if they land too far from the centre.
- A boxer must make timely decisions to dodge, defend and attack.

EXAMPLES

Team sports:
- A rugby player with the ball must decide whether to pass, kick or run.
- A batter in cricket must react to the ball and choose an appropriate shot to play.
- A volleyball player must decide if it is better to set the ball for a teammate or hit it over the net.

I'm good at dribbling — especially when I fall asleep on the couch...

You'll need to show strategies, tactics, compositional ideas, creativity and good decision-making in your two selected activities. Perfecting these things takes practice, so grab some kit and get participating.

Unit R185 — Topic Area 1: Components of Performance

Managing Performance

A performance does not always go to plan, so performers need to manage their emotions and keep focus.

Pressure can Affect Performance

1) Your arousal level is how mentally and physically alert you are.
2) To perform well you need to have the right arousal level.

If your arousal is:
- too low, you may feel bored or distracted, which can lead to poor performance.
- too high, you may feel anxious and nervous, or become too aggressive.

3) Performers can come under pressure in certain situations, which can lead to over-arousal.

EXAMPLES
- A triple jumper who has made two illegal jumps will feel more pressure on their final attempt.
- A golfer missing an easy putt could get angry with themselves.
- A tennis player could feel anxious after faulting for many serves in a row.

There are Ways for Performers to Maintain Focus

1) Performers can lower their arousal and maintain focus during performance.
2) There are lots of different techniques that exist. Here are a few examples:

- **Mental rehearsal** is imagining how your muscles feel when performing a skill.
- **Visualisation** is imagining what your performance should look like.
- **Deep breathing** can lower your heart rate and make you feel more calm.

Now remember to stay focused on the game.

Some skills need low arousal, e.g. catching a ball in cricket. But your arousal level shouldn't be too low — or you won't be alert to get into a good position.

Team Players Need Awareness of Other Performers

1) Many team sports have specific positions, which each have a different role in the game.
2) Players will have an expectation that their teammates will perform their roles correctly.

Sport	Positions
Netball	Goal keeper, goal defence, wing defence, goal shooter, goal attack, wing attack, centre.
Futsal	Goalkeeper, defender, winger, pivot.

E.g. the role of wing defence is to stop the opposition passing into the goal circle. They are only allowed in two thirds of the court.

3) However, team players may have to adapt their role based on the performance of a teammate:

- If the usual kick-taker in rugby is injured or sent off, someone will take over this responsibility.
- If a defender in football is out of position (e.g. when attacking a corner), a midfielder will drop back to cover them.

Mentally rehearse your assessment for guaranteed success...

Individual sports can be more stressful than team sports — you have no teammates to help you if things aren't going well. Try different techniques to maintain focus to find the one that works best for you.

Unit R185 — Topic Area 1: Components of Performance

Unit R185 — Topic Area 2: Improving Performance

Identifying Strengths and Weaknesses

You'll need to identify the strengths and weaknesses of your sporting performances (see p.40-41).

These Methods can Highlight Strengths and Weaknesses

1) If you know your strengths, you can use them to your advantage in competition.
2) If you know your weaknesses, you can improve them with drills and practices (see p.44-45).
3) There are many methods to assess your performance:

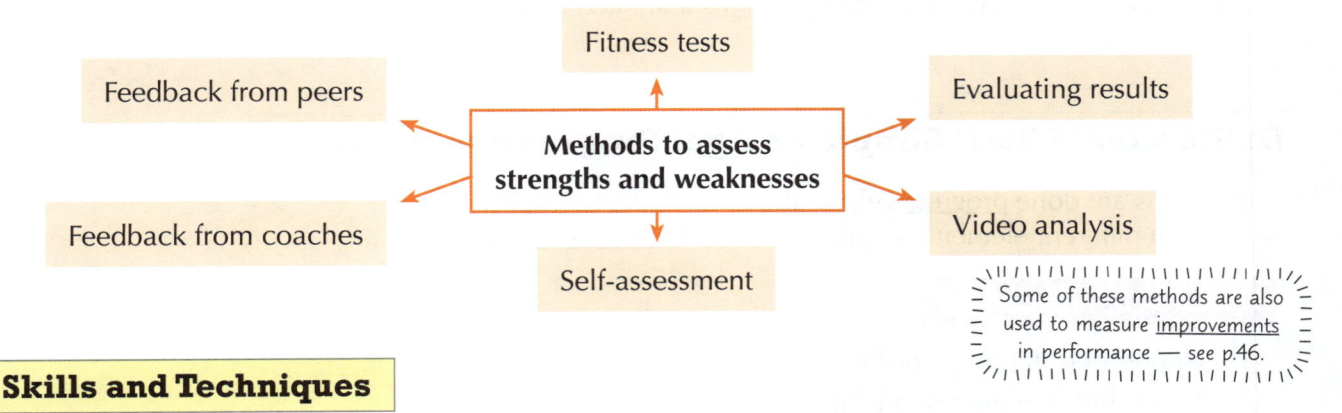

- Fitness tests
- Feedback from peers
- Feedback from coaches
- Self-assessment
- Evaluating results
- Video analysis

Methods to assess strengths and weaknesses

Some of these methods are also used to measure improvements in performance — see p.46.

Skills and Techniques

1) It is often easy to self-assess how good you are at a skill — if you can perform a skill consistently and accurately, then it is a strength. If you can't, then it is a weakness.

- Strength: you score a high proportion of the penalties you take in football.
- Weakness: you always fall over doing a handspring in gymnastics.

2) Coaches and peers can observe your performance and give feedback on your technique, e.g. that you release the javelin too early.
3) Video analysis (see p.46) can also be very useful. A skill is recorded and replayed in slow motion to identify if the technique needs improving.
4) Some basic skills can be assessed with a fitness test — these tests follow a standard procedure, which allows you to compare your results to previous results, other people and published data.

EXAMPLE
A vertical jump test shows how powerfully you can jump. The distance between two chalk marks is compared to values in a published data table to give you a result (e.g. poor, excellent).

Strategies, Tactics and Composition

1) Competition results can show if a strategy, tactic or compositional idea was successful.

- Strength: you score a 9 (out of 10) for the composition component in figure skating.
- Weakness: you conceded from each penalty corner in hockey — your tactics aren't working.

2) Coaches and peers can also observe these components and give feedback, e.g. the tactic of playing defensively in handball allowed the opponents too much possession of the ball.

An octopus is strong with forehands... and even better with eight...

Knowing your strengths and weaknesses will help you succeed in sport. It's also handy to assess your opponent's strengths and weaknesses in a game, so you can use certain tactics against them.

Improving Performance

Drills and practices are important to develop the skills and techniques needed for sport. You will need to use these methods to improve performance in your chosen activities.

Drills are Repetitive Activities to Teach Skills

1) A drill is a repetitive activity used in a training session.
2) The purpose of a drill is to train a specific skill in isolation (by itself).
3) Each sport has its own sport-specific skills that need to be mastered.

Drills should Start Simple and get Progressively Harder

Many drills are done progressively — the drill should be easy to start with, then different elements should be added to increase difficulty.

Unopposed stationary drills

1) Unopposed stationary drills break skills down to their most basic form.
2) These drills are practised while stationary (not moving).
3) Repeating this basic drill will help performers learn the correct techniques.
4) E.g. two performers stand 5 m apart and throw a rugby ball to each other.

Drills with the introduction of travel

1) You can add progression to a stationary drill with travel (movement), e.g. walking or jogging.
2) Adding travel will help performers develop more complex skills (see p.40).
3) E.g. two performers walk, keeping 5 m apart, and throw a rugby ball to each other.

Drills with passive opposition

1) Drills with passive opposition use other people as obstacles.
2) Using passive opposition in a drill means performers need to focus on what other performers are doing.
3) E.g. two performers jog, keeping 5 m apart, and throw a rugby ball to each other. Another person (passive opposition) slowly walks towards them.

The passive opposition mustn't actively interfere with the drill itself.

Drills with active opposition

1) A drill with active opposition means that an opponent is actively trying to stop the other performers from completing the drill.
2) This puts pressure on the performers and encourages them to think quickly and make decisions.
3) E.g. two performers start at the base of a triangle and another person (active opposition) starts at the top of the triangle. The performers try to get past their opponent by passing (or pretending to pass) the ball at the right time.

Unit R185 — Topic Area 2: Improving Performance

Improving Performance

There are Different Types of Practice

Whole practice — practising a whole skill from start to finish.
Used for skills that are difficult to break down into smaller parts, e.g. a golf swing.

Part practice — breaking a skill into smaller parts and practising each part separately.
Used for skills that have many different parts, e.g. a scrum in rugby.

Fixed practice

Definition: repeating a skill in the same way in an unchanging environment.

1) Fixed practice is used for skills that can be easily repeated, e.g. a sprinter setting off from the starting blocks.
2) The repetition helps you to build muscle memory and will result in you being able to use the skill without thinking about it.

Advantages:
- There's usually less pressure, which is good for beginners to gain confidence.
- Some skills can be practised without needing other people.
- Practices are often easy to explain, demonstrate and understand.

Disadvantages:
- Doing a skill in a competition is very different to doing it in practice.
- It can be boring doing the same thing repeatedly.
- It can take a lot of time to practise each skill individually.

Variable practice

Definition: repeating a skill in a variety of situations or environments.

1) Variable practice aims to recreate situations that might happen in a competition.
2) This may include drills with opposition (see previous page) or practice games.
3) You can also alter the context (change the format) of a practice game by introducing more players, experienced players or adapting the rules.
4) E.g. in netball, you could add more defenders and force players to make 5 successful passes before they shoot — this improves accurate passing skills.

You can also alter the speed of the practice — e.g. walking, jogging, then at match pace.

Advantages:
- Performers learn to perform well under pressure.
- Skills are used in a more realistic environment.
- The variety keeps training more interesting.

Disadvantages:
- Setting up variable practices can take a lot of time.
- It can be very tiring for performers.
- It often needs more people and more equipment.

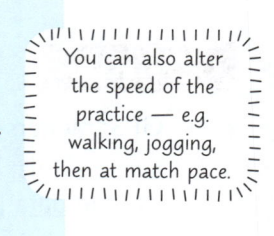

Dentists also have to do practice drills...

When planning a progressive drill, you need to think how you can take a basic skill, like throwing a ball, and add elements to increase the difficulty and improve decision-making (e.g. passive / active opposition).

Unit R185 — Topic Area 2: Improving Performance

Measuring Improvement

You can measure improvements in performance by evaluating how data changes over time.

You can Manually Track Performances...

1) A record (log book) of training or competition results may help you to spot patterns in performances.

EXAMPLE

Caitlin records her scores from three gymnastics competitions.

Apparatus	Competition 1	Competition 2	Competition 3
Vault	13.0	14.0	14.5
Beam	12.5	12.6	12.4

Her vault scores are increasing, so her skill or composition on the vault is improving.

Her beam scores are about the same — this apparatus needs more work.

2) Doing regular fitness tests can help you track fitness over time.

EXAMPLE

Bryan's training programme aims to improve his aerobic endurance.

This test measures aerobic endurance.

Fitness Test	Week 1	Week 2	Week 3	Week 4	Week 5
12-Minute Cooper Run (distance in m)	1450	1490	1530	1600	1640

His distance increases each week, so this shows his aerobic endurance is improving.

Fitness tests give quantitative (numerical) data. GPS/activity trackers (see below) also give quantitative data.

...or use Performance Analysis Technology

See p.35-37 for a reminder of other examples of technology used in sport.

Video analysis

1) Video analysis is just that — using video to analyse a performer.
2) It is used to analyse weaknesses in skills, but also tactics and strategies.
3) Video analysis software has many features, such as playing back video in slow motion, adding narration and watching two videos at the same time.

GPS Trackers

1) GPS trackers (see p.35) can measure the position and speed of a performer.
2) E.g. a cyclist can use GPS to track their efforts on a route they do often. They can use the data (e.g. speed) to analyse which part of the route they need to improve on.

Activity Trackers

1) Activity trackers (e.g. smartwatches) monitor fitness data, such as steps taken and heart rate.
2) E.g. a 5000 m runner could track their heart rate after a race. If, over time, their heart rate returns to their resting heart rate more quickly, then their aerobic endurance is improving.

Seems a tad inaccurate... 3000 steps

Keep at it — you're on the right track(er)...

When measuring improvement, you should look at the bigger picture — a performer may have a bad week and poorer results than the previous week, but their overall performance may still be improving.

Unit R185 — Topic Area 2: Improving Performance

Unit R185 — Topic Area 3: Planning Sports Activities

Planning Sports Activities

In your assessment, you will need to make a session plan for a sports activity — a good plan is clear and detailed, which will help the session run as smoothly as possible and adapt to any problems.

Participants in Sport have Different Needs

1) Activities should be planned around the needs of the participants.
2) Their needs depend on many factors, such as age, current fitness and whether they have disabilities or long-term health conditions.
3) You should use information about your participants to set goals and to influence the way that you lead your session.

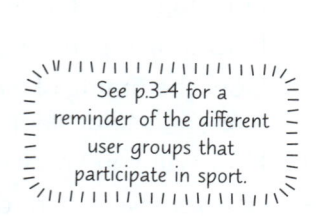

See p.3-4 for a reminder of the different user groups that participate in sport.

Think about the Venue, Equipment, Timing and Supervision

Next, you'll need to consider the following factors to organise a session:

Venue

Location
- What facilities will you need to use?
- Is the space indoors or outdoors?
- Is the space safe (e.g. clear of obstacles)?
- Will you have to share the venue with other people?
- Do you need to travel to get to the venue?
- Is the venue accessible to all participants (e.g. disability access)?

You won't always have access to the whole area, e.g. an outside pitch or sports hall.

Size
- Is the space large enough for the number of participants?
- Will you need to mark out any areas with cones or will you use lines on the floor?
- Do you need to think about vertical space (e.g. for trampolining)?

Weather
If you are using an outdoor venue...
- Is your session dependent on the weather (e.g. a nets session for cricket)?
- Can you adapt activities for different weather conditions (e.g. if it is too slippery for running)?

Equipment

- What equipment will participants need (e.g. balls, cones, bibs)?
- Do you need equipment of different sizes (e.g. a lighter discus for younger children)?
- Is there enough equipment for each participant?
- Is the equipment in good condition?
- What equipment will you need to manage participants (e.g. timer, whistle)?
- Can equipment be adjusted to meets the needs of different participants (e.g. lowering the height of hurdles)?
- Will you need to transport or store any equipment?

Planning Sports Activities

Timing

- How <u>long</u> will the <u>overall session</u> be?
- How long will each <u>part</u> of the <u>session</u> be (e.g. warm-up, drills, variable practice)?
- Does the timing of each activity <u>allow for progression</u> (e.g. <u>drills</u> to develop <u>simple skills</u> into <u>complex skills</u>)?
- How will you know <u>when to move on</u> to the next activity?
- Can you avoid periods of <u>inactivity</u>?

Flick back to p.44-45 for more on drills and practices.

You'll equally need time to revisit easier drills if participants struggle with the harder drills.

Supervision

- How <u>many participants</u> do you have?
- How <u>experienced</u> are they?
- Will participants work <u>individually</u> or in <u>groups</u>?
- How will you <u>get participants into groups</u>?
- What <u>size</u> will each group be?

What super vision these give me!

- Do you need <u>help</u> from another <u>coach</u>?
- Could an <u>experienced participant</u> help <u>supervise</u> activities?
- Do some participants require <u>additional supervision</u>?
- Does the <u>activity</u> affect the supervision required (e.g. beginner <u>swimmers</u> need <u>more supervision</u> than elite <u>hockey</u> players)?

It is recommended that <u>two adults</u> are always present for sessions with children, and <u>younger children</u> will need a <u>greater level</u> of supervision.

There are often <u>guidelines</u> for the <u>ratio</u> of adults to children, e.g. UK Athletics suggests:
- 8-12 years: <u>1 adult</u> for every <u>8 children</u>
- 13-18 years: <u>1 adult</u> for every <u>10 children</u>

The NGB (see p.32) for a sport may recommend different ratios, depending on the nature of the activity.

A Contingency Plan is a Backup Plan

1) Things can sometimes <u>go wrong</u> during a sports activity session.
2) This means that you need to have a <u>contingency plan</u> to allow the <u>activity to still go ahead</u>.
3) For example:

- Is there an <u>indoor space</u> you can use if the <u>weather is bad</u> (e.g. <u>indoor cricket nets</u>)?
- Can you <u>adapt</u> your <u>activities</u> if there are <u>fewer participants</u> than you expected?
- Can the session still <u>go ahead</u> if you are ill and <u>unable to make it</u>?
- Is there <u>somewhere else</u> you can go if <u>another group</u> has <u>booked</u> your venue?

I love being spontaneous, but only if it's been carefully planned...

There are many factors to consider in a session plan, and some things (e.g. bringing the bibs) might seem obvious... but a well-planned session is important so you aren't wasting time when participants arrive.

Planning Sports Activities Safely

Safety is another important part of planning sports activities. Here's what you need to know.

Doing a Risk Assessment Helps you to Take Corrective Actions

1) Risk assessments are used to help you plan a sports activity that is safe for all participants.
2) To carry out a risk assessment, list the potential hazards, stating the severity (how serious it is) and the probability (chance) of each one occurring. Then, list corrective actions to minimise (reduce) the risks.
3) For example, here is part of a risk assessment for a football session:

Hazard	Severity	Probability	How to minimise risk
The pitch could be slippery, which could lead to injuries.	Medium	High	Check participants have appropriate footwear, e.g. studded boots.
The goal could fall over and hit someone.	Low	Low	Secure the goal correctly.
Extreme heat could cause dehydration and exhaustion.	High	Medium	Allow for regular breaks and provide access to drinking water.

Checking Equipment and Clothing can Prevent Injuries

1) It's important to check all equipment and clothing is safe before using it.
2) This includes activity-specific equipment (e.g. nets are properly secured and at the correct height) and safety equipment (e.g. a cricket helmet is undamaged).
3) Jewellery should be removed or covered and long hair should be tied back.
4) You should also clear the playing area and surrounding area of any obstructions.

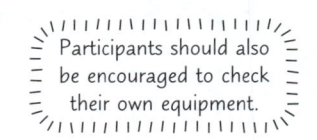

Participants should also be encouraged to check their own equipment.

First Aid Equipment is Necessary to Treat Injuries

1) Injuries in sport are common, even when you have reduced the risks.
2) So, there must be a well-stocked first aid kit available and at least one person with a basic first aid qualification to quickly deal with any injuries.

> You must have an Emergency Action Plan (EAP) in place in case of an emergency, and know the correct procedures to follow. An EAP should include:
> - the contact details of a qualified first aider
> - emergency contact numbers (e.g. 999) and the location of a telephone
> - the location of the first aid kit

You Must be Aware of Child Protection Issues

1) Children are vulnerable and everyone has a responsibility to protect them from harm. Safeguarding in sport is about providing a safe environment for everyone to participate in sport.
2) However, some children can suffer from abuse (e.g. physical, emotional or sexual abuse).
3) If you have any concerns about the welfare of a child, you should report it to an appropriate authority, such as the National Governing Body of the sport, or the police.

Here's a safety tip for Halloween — wear a mask...
Safety during a sports activity doesn't just extend to the participants. It's also about keeping coaches, volunteer staff, spectators and the general public safe (if the session is happening in a public area).

Unit R185 — Topic Area 3: Planning Sports Activities

Planning Activities to Meet Objectives

Every session plan should include clear objectives (goals) and activities that set out to meet those objectives.

Objectives Should be SMART

S	Specific →	A participant should know exactly what they want to achieve, e.g. 'My goal is to swim 1000 m continuously'.
M	Measurable →	Goals need to be measurable, so participants can see progress, e.g. 'My goal is to run 100 m in under 12 seconds'.
A	Achievable →	The goal should be at the right level of difficulty. If it is too easy, it won't be motivating. If it is too difficult, a participant may give up.
R	Realistic →	A participant needs to have everything to reach their goal — e.g. the right level of fitness and skill, or enough resources (time, facilities...).
T	Time-bound →	Set a deadline for reaching a goal. This makes the target measurable and keeps a performer motivated.

Each Session Should Start with an Introduction

1) Before a session starts, you should introduce yourself to the participants.
2) You should first explain what the objectives for the session are, e.g. learning how to serve in tennis.
3) You should then do some safety checks (see p.49) — this includes a review of your risk assessment and checking participants are injury-free and have appropriate clothing and safety equipment.

An Effective Warm-Up is Essential

A warm-up helps to prepare participants' bodies for exercise. It typically takes 10-15 minutes. It should involve:

A pulse raiser — activity that gradually increases in intensity to increase the heart rate.
- This eases the body into exercising and increases the oxygen supply to the muscles. It warms up muscles and makes them more elastic, which reduces the chance of injury.
- Pulse raiser activities includes things like jogging, skipping or cycling.

Stretching and mobility exercises — activities that increase flexibility and mobility of muscles. It should focus on the muscles and movements used in the activity. There are two types of stretch:

Static stretches — stretches performed without moving, e.g. standing quadriceps stretch.

Dynamic stretches — stretches performed with movement, e.g. lunges or high kicks.

Practice actions / skill rehearsal — e.g. practice shots or throwing and catching.
- This prepares the muscles that will be used in the activity, so they perform better.
- It also helps participants focus on the activity ahead (see p.42 for mental preparation).

Unit R185 — Topic Area 3: Planning Sports Activities

Planning Activities to Meet Objectives

The Main Activity Focuses on Developing Skills and Techniques

1) The objective of any sports activity session is to improve the skills and techniques of participants.
2) The main activity will typically begin with a skill in its basic form. New elements are added to drills as participants become more confident — e.g. adding travel and opposition.

   Adding progression to drills was covered on p.44.

3) This progression of a skill helps to keep the session interesting for participants. This keeps them motivated, especially if they start to find the basic skill easy to perform.
4) However, participants won't always progress at the same level. Some participants may need to continue working on a basic skill or technique for longer than others.
5) Often, the main activity will end with some variable practice (p.45), so participants have to adapt to performing the skill in a more realistic environment.

Cool-Downs Help Your Body Return to a Resting State

A cool-down should be performed after the main activity. A cool-down gradually decreases in intensity to return the body to resting levels. It should involve:

Low-intensity exercise — gentle exercise, like jogging, keeps the heart and lungs working harder than normal. The intensity is gradually reduced (e.g. from a jog to walking).
- Gradually reducing the intensity allows your heart rate, breathing rate and body temperature to decrease gradually back to their resting levels.
- It helps to remove the waste products of exercise, such as carbon dioxide and lactic acid.

Stretching — muscles used in the activity are stretched to speed up recovery and improve flexibility.
- Stretching while the muscles are warm helps to improve flexibility.
- It may also help to reduce muscle stiffness and fatigue in the muscles.

You Should Always End Each Session with a Conclusion

1) Gather all the participants around at the end of the session and thank them for coming.
2) It's a good idea to recap the objectives that were achieved during the session and ask open questions to check what the participants have learned.
3) You could also give information about the next session, e.g. when it will be and what the objectives are.
4) Giving participants praise at the end of the session (for the effort they've put in) will encourage them to come back for the next one.

Hysterical pun on 'objective' has failed to load...

It's really important to have clear objectives in mind before you plan a sports activity session. Once you've decided on the objectives, you can create activities and drills that work towards achieving those objectives.

Unit R185 — Topic Area 3: Planning Sports Activities

Organising Sports Activities

Showing good organisation skills is essential to deliver a safe and suitable sports activity session. This page will focus on one sport (cricket) to show you the things that you'll need to consider.

Safe Practice Means Making Sure Everyone is Safe

1) The safety of participants at your sports activity session is your responsibility.
2) This means your participants and activities must be organised depending on the venue, number of participants and the equipment being used.
3) For example, a net session for cricket would be unsafe with lots of participants. Instead, you could divide the participants into smaller groups. One group could work in the nets while the other groups do fielding drills.

Have a Set Amount of Time for Each Activity

The length of your session will vary depending on the sport and the experience of the group. For example, here is how you might organise an hour-long cricket fielding session for beginners:

Activity	Duration	Description
Intro	5 minutes	Explain the objectives of the session.
Warm-up	10 minutes	Pulse raiser, stretches and skill rehearsal.
Drills	35 minutes	Catching, throwing, stopping the ball.
Cool-down	5 minutes	Light jogging and stretches.
Conclusion	5 minutes	Give feedback on overall session.

See p.50-51 for more on warm-ups and cool-downs.

Your Activities Need to be Adaptable

1) Adaptability means changing an activity to suit the needs of the participants.
2) Some activities will need to be adapted if participants are finding them too easy or too difficult.
3) For example, this is how you could adapt a cricket drill where participants throw the ball at the stumps:

Making the drill easier (regression)
- Move participants closer to the stumps, making the throw shorter.
- Change the angle of the stumps so the participants have a full view of all three stumps.

Making the drill harder (progression) 
- Move participants further away from the stumps, making them put more effort into their throw.
- Change the angle of the stumps so the participants only have one stump to aim at.

Reliability will Earn Respect with your Participants

1) Reliability means that you always start and finish the session on time and you keep participants informed about what's going on.
2) Make sure that you arrive at the session before everyone else to set up for your activities.
3) Being a reliable leader will also encourage your participants to be more reliable.

How do netball players stay cool? They sit next to their fans...
Make sure that you're familiar with all the organisation skills you need before moving on to the next page. Some skills, like adaptability and reliability, aren't always easy — but should come with more experience.

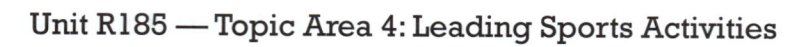

Leading Sports Activities

You've done all the planning and organising of a sports activity session... and now it's time to actually lead it.

A Successful Leader Needs to Show Certain Qualities

As the leader of a sports activity session, it's important to take overall responsibility for the session and your participants. A successful leader will have many qualities, which will develop over time:

- You follow a well-organised session plan (see p.47-52) and can adapt it when things are not going to plan.
- You keep your participants safe at all times (see p.49).
- You adapt your leadership style to suit the needs of the group (see below).
- You show strong communication skills and motivate participants (see p.54).
- You show confidence and have great knowledge of your sport (see p.55).

These are also the qualities you'll need to show in your assessment for top marks.

How does this help my front crawl, coach?

Each Activity Should be Specific to the Sport

1) Each activity in a session should always be made relevant to the sport:

- Warm-ups should use the same equipment, movements and muscles as the sport. E.g. cyclists could use an indoor exercise bike for the pulse raiser.

- Drills should focus on the specific skills, techniques or tactics required for the sport. E.g. footballers could work on set piece plays on a football pitch.

2) Activities should also be at an appropriate level for the participants, e.g. teaching how to perform a forehand stroke in tennis is suitable for beginners, but not for experienced performers.

There are Three Different Leadership Styles

1) There are different approaches you can take to lead a group.

A democratic style of leadership is known as a 'person-oriented' style.

Democratic

- A democratic leader asks participants for their opinions and then makes a decision.
- For example, you could ask participants in a hockey session whether they want to focus on shooting, dribbling or passing. You then pick the activity that was most popular.

Autocratic

This is a 'task-oriented' style.

- An autocratic leader decides what to do without asking for the opinions of participants.
- For example, you decide to focus on tackling in a rugby session, and no-one else gets to make a decision.

Laissez-faire

- A laissez-faire leader has a laid-back style — they let the participants get on with activities without getting involved or giving much feedback.
- For example, you let participants play a lacrosse practice game by themselves. You observe them but don't give much feedback until after the game.

2) The leadership style you choose should depend on the needs of the group.
3) Beginners may benefit from an autocratic leader because they are new to the sport and will require guidance on the correct techniques to use.
4) Experienced performers may want to feel more involved in their own development — a democratic leader would be the best option for these performers.

Unit R185 — Topic Area 4: Leading Sports Activities

Leading Sports Activities

Leaders Have Their Own Delivery Style

1) Delivery style is about how a leader actually runs a sports activity session.
2) There are two main delivery styles:

Proactive delivery style
- A proactive delivery style means that the leader has planned the entire session.
- The plan would include solutions to any problems that might pop up, e.g. what to do if only half of the participants attend the session.

Reactive delivery style
- A reactive delivery style means that the leader adapts their session according to the situation.
- For example, they could simplify a dance routine if participants are struggling with some of the skills.

Leaders Must Have Strong Communication Skills

1) The position of the leader is very important — when you explain or demonstrate (see below) a skill or drill, you should position yourself so that:

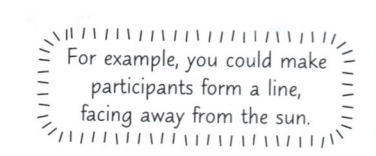

- all participants can see you.
- you can see all participants.

For example, you could make participants form a line, facing away from the sun.

2) Communicating clearly is also very important when leading a sports activity session.
3) The way you communicate will depend on the needs of the group.
E.g. you should use simpler words and fewer technical terms with younger children.

Verbal communication
- This means using your voice to communicate with participants.
- You should speak clearly, loudly and concisely.

Non-verbal communication
- This means communicating without speaking.
- You could use gestures (with arms and hands) or facial expressions.

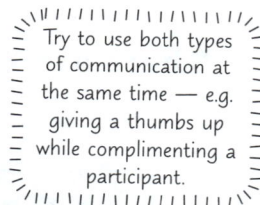

Try to use both types of communication at the same time — e.g. giving a thumbs up while complimenting a participant.

Demonstrating Shows Participants How it Should be Done

1) Demonstrating a skill or drill is usually better than just explaining it.
2) It shows the participants exactly what they need to do and how they need to do it.
3) Demonstrations can be done by a leader or skilled participant, or a video can be watched.
4) Demonstrations are particularly important for children or beginners learning a new skill, who may need visual aids to understand what to do.
5) Here are some important things you should do when demonstrating:

- Do the demonstration slowly
- Repeat the demonstration several times
- Make sure everyone can see

- Break down each part of the skill
- Get performers to copy your movements
- Answer any questions

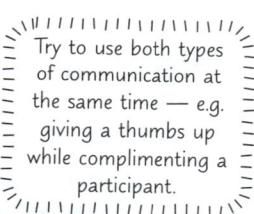

Unit R185 — Topic Area 4: Leading Sports Activities

Leading Sports Activities

Leaders Need to be Able to Motivate Participants

1) Motivation is about how keen you are to do something. It's what drives you on when things get difficult — your desire to succeed.
2) Motivation can be either intrinsic (from within yourself) or extrinsic (from outside).

Intrinsic Motivation
Motivation from the enjoyment and good feelings you get when taking part in physical activity and sport, e.g. pride, high self-esteem.

Extrinsic Motivation
Motivation through rewards from other people/sources. This can be tangible (you can touch it, e.g. trophies, money) or intangible (you can't touch it, e.g. applause, praise from a coach).

3) When leading a session, you should show enthusiasm for the activity and look to give immediate positive feedback (praise) to support any good techniques and effort...
4) ...and constructive (or corrective) feedback on specific areas for participants to improve.
5) Showing enthusiasm and giving useful feedback will help to keep a participant motivated.

You Need to Show Confidence as a Leader

1) To be a good leader, you need to be confident in your own ability to lead a session.
2) Participants will trust you as a leader if you show confidence and back your own decisions.
3) Some sessions may not go as planned, but you will learn and improve your skills each time. The more sessions you lead, the easier it gets, and the more confident you will become.
4) If there are areas in your leadership that you feel need improving, ask other leaders and coaches for feedback on your performance.

A Creative Approach to Activities Makes them More Fun

1) Being creative will help to keep sessions interesting for participants and keep them engaged.
2) Try to avoid doing the same drills every session. If you do repeat a drill, you can still be creative and add different elements to it.

EXAMPLE

Fielding drill — cricket
- Don't put participants in one line and give each of them a catch — this will get boring.
- Instead, place two cones 15 m apart and have participants form a line behind each cone.
- Then, place yourself about 20 m away from the cones and hit a ball (along the ground or in the air) between the two cones.
- The participants at the front of each line must quickly decide who fields and catches the ball.
- This makes the drill more interesting and encourages participants to communicate.

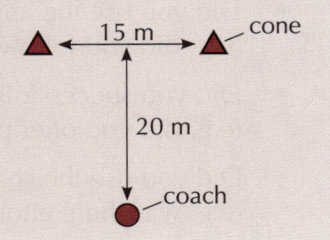

Good rugby leaders can tackle any challenge that comes their way...

These pages offer tips on being a successful leader, but it's more important to get out there and start leading sports activity sessions yourself. That's the only way to start building and improving your leadership skills.

Unit R185 — Topic Area 4: Leading Sports Activities

Reviewing Activity Planning

The last pages in this unit cover reviewing your own performance in planning and leading a session.

Reflect on Your Performance After a Session

1) After leading a sports activity session, it is useful to reflect and self-assess how it went.
2) You might also gather feedback from your participants.
3) You should review your session plan and leadership, identifying what was successful (positives) and what didn't go well (negatives).
4) This information will help you to take action to improve your planning and delivering of sessions in the future (see next page) and become a more confident leader.

Reviewing your Session Plan

A good session plan (see p.47-51) describes how you will use the venue and equipment. It should include timings for each activity and explain how to organise the participants.

- Was your plan easy to follow?
  (e.g. did your plan make sense when you followed it in the session?)
- Did you have enough equipment for the group?
  (e.g. were people waiting for equipment to be free?)
- Did you plan your activities in a suitable order?
  (e.g. was there a clear progression of skills from start to finish?)
- Were the activities suitable for the level of the group?
  (e.g. were any activities too easy or too hard?)
- Did you adapt activities for different abilities within the group?
  (e.g. did you give extra help to those who needed it?)
- Did you show creativity in your session?
  (e.g. did you adapt any drills to make them more engaging?)

Reviewing your Leadership

A strong leader should be positive, confident and be able to adapt to any unexpected situations.

- Did you carry out the session safely?
  (e.g. did you check for injuries and review your risk assessment?)

  You should make changes to your risk assessment (see p.49) if you need to.

- Did you use the appropriate amount of time on each activity?
  (e.g. did you follow the timings on your plan?)
- Did you successfully motivate the group?
  (e.g. did you offer praise and constructive feedback?)
- Did you use the space effectively?
  (e.g. was there enough room for each activity?)
- Did you adapt the session if things didn't go to plan?
  (e.g. were some drills too difficult?)

  You might have referred to your contingency plan (see p.48).

- Did you position yourself to communicate effectively?
  (e.g. were you able to see the group at all times?)

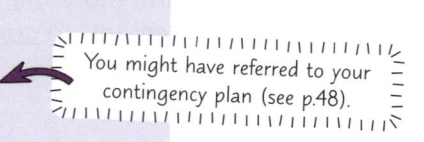

Planning Improvements

Identify Areas to Improve the Next Session

You should use your review to suggest improvements to make your next session even better. Take a look at this example:

EXAMPLE

Session plan for gymnastics

- Warm-up (10 minutes) — play 'traffic lights' as a pulse raiser, then stretches and jumps on the floor
- Drills on beam (20 minutes) — basic walks, straight jumps, tuck jumps, star jumps, wolf jumps
- Practice competition (15 minutes) — combine jumps to make a routine
- Cool-down (5 minutes) — light jogging and stretches

Children jog when 'green' is said, walk on 'amber' and do a balance on 'red'.

Participants: 10 children (Year 5)
Level: mixed abilities
Objective: Perform basic travels and jumps on the beam.
Equipment: 1 × beam, 2 × crash mats

Positives	Negatives
• I was loud and clear with my instructions during the warm-up. • I was positioned well, as I could see the whole group at all times. • There was a good progression of skills — from basic walking to performing jumps in a pretend competition. • The gymnasts found it motivating to judge each other's routines.	• I took longer in the warm-up than I had planned, so I could only spend 15 minutes on the drills. • I only had access to one beam, so gymnasts had to wait for their turn. • I verbally explained what a wolf jump was, but the group didn't understand. • Some gymnasts found the main drills too easy, and got bored quite quickly.

Improvements for the next session:

1) Keep a close eye on time so that each part of the session takes the planned amount of time.
2) Set out benches so gymnasts can practise jumps while they wait for the beam to be free.
3) Demonstrate skills, particularly those that are complicated to verbally explain (e.g. wolf jumps).
4) Adapt drills by adding obstacles (e.g. hoops) to increase difficulty for gymnasts with higher ability.

Look Out for Opportunities to Improve Your Leadership Skills

1) To be a successful leader in sport, you should take opportunities to develop your skills.
2) This might involve:

   - taking a coaching or leadership course organised by your sport's NGB.
   - volunteering at a local sports club to gain more experience.
   - helping teachers with extra-curricular sports activities.

Nope, can't think of a single thing to improve about myself...

In the assessment, you'll need to evaluate (review) your own sports activity session. For top marks, you should give detailed positives and negatives and justify how you would adapt your plan for future sessions.

Unit R185 — Topic Area 5: Reviewing Activity Planning

Sport and the Media

There are lots of different ways that sport is covered in the media, including digital, broadcast and print media.

Digital and Social Media Mean Fans can Watch Sport Anywhere

1) Digital and social media are popular ways of accessing sports coverage.
2) These sources are accessible for most people, but appeal to younger fans especially.
3) Smartphones and tablets allow people to access this sports coverage on the move.
4) There are different categories of digital and social media:

Website — pages of content on the World Wide Web, which you access using the internet. Sports websites, e.g. Sky Sports or BBC Sport, list results and sports news.

Blog — an informal website, a bit like a journal, which is regularly updated by individuals or small groups. Content appears in reverse order, with the latest post appearing first. Sports blogs include RaceFans (for motorsport news) and caughtoffside (for football news).

Social networking platform — a website or app where users create a profile and connect with other users, e.g. Facebook or Instagram. Fans communicate using text, photos or videos and can share trending sports news and gossip.

   1) Many football teams use social networking platforms to reach their fans, e.g. Manchester United FC has millions of followers on Instagram.
   2) Individual players also have a huge following — Cristiano Ronaldo was the most-followed person on Instagram in 2022.

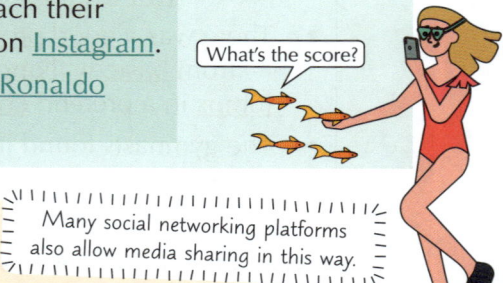

Media sharing platform — a website or app designed for users to post and share photos or videos, e.g. Pinterest or TikTok. Fans can upload and share sports content, such as trick shots and goal compilations.

Many social networking platforms also allow media sharing in this way.

Live streaming platform — a website or app which broadcasts an event live, e.g. TWITCH or YouTube TV™ service. A community sports club may broadcast a sports event this way.

5) There are advantages and disadvantages of digital and social media covering sport.

Advantages and Disadvantages:

Advantages:
- Sports coverage is accessible almost anywhere, due to smartphones.
- Social media allows performers to create fun content and build a personal brand.
- Opportunity for interaction between performers and their fans, which builds loyalty.
- Live streaming is often a cheaper way to watch a sporting event live.

Disadvantages:
- Social media posts can be inaccurate or controversial, which can damage the reputation of a team or sport.
- Negative comments can impact performers and put pressure on them to perform well.
- People may become more interested in the lives of performers than the sport itself.
- Live streaming may mean fewer people watch sport in person.

What's the score?

Sport and the Media

Broadcast Media Includes TV, Radio and Podcasts

1) Broadcast media is a more traditional way of keeping up to date with sport.
2) There are three main forms of broadcast media:

TV

- Modern TVs come with Freeview — hundreds of channels that can be watched for free, including those run by the BBC and ITV.
- The government has listed some sporting events that must always be available to watch live on TV for free, including the Olympic Games and Wimbledon.
- Smart TVs can connect to the internet, so have many more features than a traditional TV.
- They can access subscription channels, such as Sky Sports or TNT Sports (originally BT Sport). These channels offer a wider range of live sports, but have subscription fees.

Households in the UK need to pay for a TV licence to watch any live TV, even on Freeview.

Subscription channels are also available on satellite and cable TV.

Radio

- Radio allows people to listen to live sporting events, news and debates.
- National radio stations cover major sporting events, e.g. BBC Radio 5 Live is a popular radio station that provides live commentary of Premier League football games.
- Local radio stations cover local sports news and provide match commentaries — many of these are provided by the BBC.
- DAB (digital audio broadcasting) radio is transmitted digitally rather than using radio waves. This gives it a better sound quality. talkSPORT is a popular DAB radio station.
- Internet radio stations can be accessed through the internet. Many popular radio stations also broadcast online, including BBC Radio 5 Live and talkSPORT.

Podcasts

- Podcasts are audio recordings of discussions, debates and reactions to events or news that can be downloaded or streamed, e.g. That Peter Crouch Podcast.
- They are available on lots of different platforms, including BBC Sounds, Spotify® and Amazon Music.

Some podcasts are available as videos.

3) Broadcast media is able to reach a wide audience — most people have access to a TV or radio. It appeals to casual viewers as well as loyal fans.
4) Here are the advantages and disadvantages of this type of media:

Advantages and Disadvantages:

Advantages:
- Radio programmes and podcasts can be listened to anywhere using a smartphone.
- A wide variety of content is available.
- Most content is available for free.

Disadvantages:
- There is a subscription fee to access some TV programmes.
- Broadcasting live games reduces in-person attendance.
- Only the wealthiest companies can afford to spend huge amounts of money for the rights to broadcast popular live events.

Unit R186 — Topic Area 1: Sporting Media Sources

Sport and the Media

Print Media is Newspapers, Magazines and Books

1) Print media is another traditional method of covering sport.
2) There are three main types:

Newspapers

- Newspapers usually cover sports news and match summaries.
- Broadsheet newspapers, e.g. The Guardian, are more informative and cover a wider range of sports.
- Tabloids, e.g. The Daily Mail, tend to focus on more sensational topics and people, making their news stories accessible and with a wide appeal. They tend to cover the most popular sports.

Magazines

- Magazines may cover news across all sports, or focus on a specific sport, e.g. The Cricketer.
- They are usually published weekly or monthly and fans pay a subscription fee.

Books

- Books about sport can be fiction (made up) or non-fiction (factual).
- Non-fiction books may cover general information about a sport, such as the history of the sport.
- Other non-fiction books include skill books, which explain how certain skills should be performed. They are useful for beginners or people trying to improve a specific skill.
- Fans can also buy their favourite performer's autobiography, e.g. 'Gloves Off' by Tyson Fury.

For more on skills, see p.40.

3) Some forms of print media are suitable for people with limited knowledge of a sport, such as an introductory book or article, but other forms of print media are aimed at dedicated fans, such as monthly magazines.
4) There are advantages and disadvantages of print media:

Advantages and Disadvantages:

Advantages:
- You don't need technology to access print media.
- There is a wide variety of content available.
- Information in books is usually more accurate than some online sources.

Disadvantages:
- Magazine subscriptions can be expensive.
- There's no way of accessing live results.
- Information in books may not always be up-to-date.

I like the sound of print media...
In the assessment, you'll research and compare the different media sources that could help promote a sports club or activity — make sure you use current examples of digital/social, broadcast and print media.

Positive Effects of the Media in Sport

Media coverage has lots of positive effects for sports, performers and the general population...

The Media Helps to Increase Participation and Remove Barriers

1) Media coverage makes more people aware of different sports, which means more people are encouraged to take part.
2) Major sporting events (see p.24) bring in large numbers of spectators — these events influence participation. For example:

EXAMPLES
- Participation in cycling increased after the GB cycling team won 12 medals at the London 2012 Olympics.
- Tennis centres see a big rise in the number of people booking courts when Wimbledon is on the TV.

3) Media coverage can also remove some barriers to participation (p.5-7). For example, if minority groups see people of the same ethnicity or background as themselves represented in sport, they are more likely to participate.

Coverage of Performers Creates Role Models...

1) The media increases the exposure of sports performers.
2) Many successful performers are viewed as role models by the general public — these performers can inspire people to participate or achieve their goals.
3) Sometimes these performers can become 'influencers' through social media.

EXAMPLES
- Marcus Rashford has gained a large following on social media through playing for Manchester United FC. He has used his influence to campaign for free school meals and books for disadvantaged children.
- Nicola Adams became the first woman to win an Olympic medal in boxing at the London 2012 Olympics. She has inspired women and girls to take up sports that are stereotyped as being only suitable for men.

...and Helps to Raise the Profile of Sport

1) Media coverage can draw attention to specific sports.
2) Initiatives and campaigns can be promoted using all media sources, and are often made more successful by partnerships with celebrities or role models.

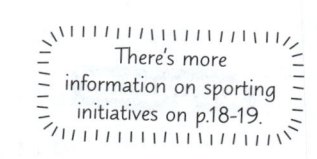

There's more information on sporting initiatives on p.18-19.

EXAMPLES
- In 2022, the Lawn Tennis Association (LTA) launched the 'Play Your Way' campaign — various films were made to promote tennis as an inclusive sport.
- The 2021 'Your Netball World' campaign celebrated individuality within netball.
- The Golf Foundation's 'Golf Is Ours' campaign aimed to encourage schools to teach golf by providing free resources. The campaign was supported by former professional golfer, Nick Dougherty.

Positive Effects of the Media in Sport

Active, Healthy Lifestyles can be Promoted in the Media

1) Online promotions and social media encourage more people to be interested in health and fitness.
2) People are increasingly thinking about how they can keep active at home.
3) There are now lots of fitness classes available online — these can be live or on demand.
4) Some of these are free through websites or apps, but others require a subscription.

EXAMPLES
- Joe Wicks has a huge range of fitness classes available on his YouTube™ video community channel. He has workouts specifically aimed at beginners, and encourages people of all fitness levels to get active.
- THIS GIRL CAN is a national campaign that aims to encourage women and girls to get active, regardless of their ability or background.

Emerging Sports can also be Promoted

1) Media coverage provides exposure for new and emerging sports (p.13). This raises the awareness of a sport and can make it more popular.
2) The wide range of sports TV channels, websites, podcasts and magazines available means that people are far more likely to hear or read about emerging sports.

EXAMPLES
- Newspaper and social media coverage has provided lots of exposure for walking football, which has become increasingly popular. It encourages over 50s, people recovering from injuries and people of lower mobility to participate in a team sport.
- Skateboarding first became an Olympic sport at the Tokyo 2020 Olympics. The exposure gained from this major event has given the sport credibility, and Sky Brown became Team GB's youngest ever medal winner, making her a role model for young girls.

The Media Helps People Learn About Changes to Sport

1) The media provides a platform where changes to existing sports can be explained.
2) Pundits can break down and analyse games for viewers or readers.
3) Changes may be to the rules of a specific sport, or can involve new variations, formats or technology.

EXAMPLES
- The FA post each year's key rule changes on their website in a simplified format, to make it easier for fans to understand.
- 'Safe standing' areas were introduced in football stadiums for the 2022/23 Premier League season. Media coverage meant more people were aware of this.
- In 2023, the AELTC (All England Lawn Tennis Club) announced that the men's doubles format at Wimbledon would change from best-of-five to best-of-three sets. Media coverage provided exposure for this significant change.
- Smart balls (balls with microchips that provide data on position) were used at the 2023 Six Nations. Media coverage helped explain this new technology to fans.

Unit R186 — Topic Area 2: Positive Effects of the Media in Sport

Positive Effects of the Media in Sport

Revenue Means How Much Money is Made

1) People can make money (revenue) through sport. Revenue comes from different sources, including lottery grants, sponsorships, ticket sales, merchandise and the media.
2) Sport is a commodity (product) and people who own or invest in clubs or events can influence sport as a whole. For example, players in the top football leagues are bought and sold for millions of pounds.
3) The huge amount of money involved has led to the creation of roles such as sports promoters and agents.

Sport, the Media and Sponsorship are All Connected

Sport, the media and sponsorship have grown to depend on one another — this is called the 'golden triangle'.

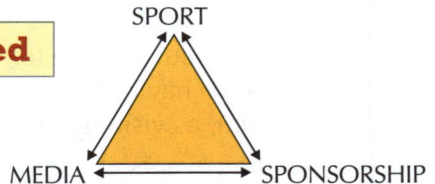

The Media and Sport

1) Media companies use sport to promote themselves so that more people use their products or services, e.g. buy their newspapers or watch their TV / subscription channels.
2) Sports performers and teams use the media to promote themselves by advertising upcoming events and building an online presence (see p.58). Media coverage can lead to increases in ticket and merchandise sales.
3) Money also comes directly from media companies, as they pay to cover sport as entertainment.
4) Some sports change their rules or adapt competitions to gain more media coverage:

EXAMPLE
Twenty20 Cricket was created to make a more fast-paced, exciting version of cricket that would attract a higher number of spectators.

Sponsorship and Sport

1) Sponsorship deals mean companies can associate their name with successful sports performers and teams. This is an effective form of advertising, which helps the sponsor make more money.
2) These deals mean big money for sport — which can be spent on new stadiums or higher wages, which benefits the players and spectators.

EXAMPLES
- Arthur J. Gallagher & Co. (an insurance company) became sponsors of Premiership Rugby in 2018, so it became known as the Gallagher Premiership.
- NIKE provided the kit for England's national team in the UEFA Women's EURO 2022.
- British tennis player Andy Murray wore clothing by Castore after signing a deal in 2019.

Sponsorship and Media

1) The more media coverage a sport gets, the more people watch it. This makes the sponsorship more valuable, as it can reach a larger audience.
2) Performers can demand more money for sponsorship deals in sports with a wide audience.

Why's he playing?
His dad sponsors the team.

CGP CGP CGP CGP (CGP — Official Sponsors of page 63)...
You'll need to write about a sports club's relationship with the media in your assessment, so make sure you know the different positive effects. It's a good idea to find some examples relevant to your sport.

Unit R186 — Topic Area 2: Positive Effects of the Media in Sport

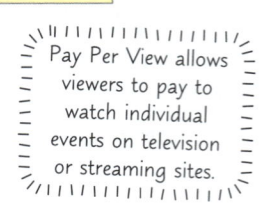

Negative Effects of the Media in Sport

There are also many ways that the media can negatively impact those who are involved in sport.

Media Coverage Means Fewer People Watch Sport In Person

1) Live streaming, Pay Per View (PPV) and social networking have made sport cheaper and more convenient to watch at home. This can reduce the number of spectators who attend sporting events in person.
2) The atmosphere of live sporting events can suffer as a result. Emptier stadiums are less fun for spectators, and mean there is a lack of support for sports performers.
3) This is particularly true for 'away' games, where watching at home also avoids having to travel. This can affect the communities surrounding a stadium, as visiting fans would usually spend money in the local area.
4) Watching events at home can also lead to gambling, which can become an addiction. Targeted ads for gambling sites can appear on TV channels, streaming sites and social media.

Pay Per View allows viewers to pay to watch individual events on television or streaming sites.

Scheduling can be Changed to Benefit the Media

1) The media can influence the number of games played or the timings of matches — schedules are changed so that more matches can be shown or start times are changed to draw the largest audience possible.
2) Busier schedules mean players have less time to rest, so there is more risk of injury.

EXAMPLES

- Premier League football has a busier schedule between Christmas and New Year. This benefits the media as people are more likely to watch at home, but means many spectators won't be able to attend games in person. It can also be exhausting for players.
- The number of teams at the Men's FIFA World Cup™ has increased from 32 to 48, meaning more matches and more revenue, but more intense schedules for the players.

Many People Question Whether some Sponsors are Ethical

1) Some sports and events are sponsored by tobacco, alcohol, gambling or junk food companies.
2) Excessive consumption of junk food and alcohol can be dangerous, while gambling may become an addiction for some people.
3) Due to these concerns, many people question whether these companies should be associated with sport because of the unhealthy lifestyle they can encourage — arguing it is unethical (morally wrong).

EXAMPLES

- Formula One teams have a history of advertising tobacco companies on their cars. This was banned in 2005, but tobacco companies can still invest in Formula One teams.
- The American National Football League (NFL) has sponsorships deals with various alcohol companies, which means they can sell their drinks at events.
- 8 of the 20 teams in the 2022/2023 Premier League season were sponsored by gambling companies — their logos could be seen on players' shirts.
- The Hundred (a cricket tournament) faced criticism for partnering with a snacks company.
- Diet and supplement products are often promoted by sportspeople on social media.

4) The behaviour of the sponsor can reflect on the performer and vice versa — this means it can be damaging for both the sponsor and performer if either one receives negative media coverage.

Negative Effects of the Media in Sport

The Media Makes the Wealth Divide Worse

1) Money and exposure from the media is often only available to the top players and teams, so it doesn't benefit sport as a whole.
2) For example, Premier League football teams have more media coverage than teams in lower leagues and other sports teams, so they can demand more money for agents' fees, wages and TV rights.
3) This can create a wealth divide between popular sports and emerging sports, as emerging sports receive less revenue from the media.
4) There is also a gender divide in earnings. Women's sport attracts less sponsorship and media coverage than men's sport. This means female performers aren't paid as well as male performers, and often can't train full time.

See p.10-12 for more on the popularity of sport.

Sport is Affected by Global Issues

1) Media coverage allows people to watch sport all over the world.
2) However, this means that sport is affected by global issues.
3) The media can't cater for all spectators of an international event, because of differences in time zones.
4) For example, the men's and women's 100 m finals at the Tokyo 2020 Olympic Games could be watched during the day in the UK and US, but this meant that the performers had to compete at 9.50 pm in Tokyo.
5) Current affairs (events happening at the present time) can also affect sport and the media globally:

> During the COVID-19 pandemic, many sporting events were cancelled or spectators weren't allowed to attend. Cancelled events meant that the media couldn't promote sport, which meant less revenue for both the media and sport (see the relationship between sport and the media on p.63).

Coverage of Inappropriate Behaviour Sets a Bad Example

1) Inappropriate behaviour on-field and off-field is made more visible by media coverage.
2) Videos of poor behaviour (e.g. gamesmanship or violence) are often replayed and shared on social media, meaning they can quickly be seen by lots of people.
3) This can negatively impact the reputation of performers, teams or sports. It also goes against sporting values (see p.14-15).
4) Poor behaviour may be copied across society, e.g. aggression towards officials at amateur games and at live spectator events.

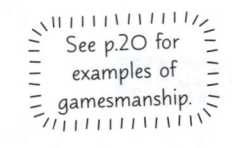

See p.20 for examples of gamesmanship.

EXAMPLES

- An assistant for Festina (a cycling team) was found with PEDs (p.22-23) before the 1998 Tour de France. This damaged the reputation of cycling.
- Saracens broke Premiership Rugby's £7 million salary cap in 2019, causing them to be fined £5.3 million and demoted from the Premiership.
- Luis Suárez was caught biting Branislav Ivanović during a football match in 2013. Suárez set a bad example to spectators and was banned for 10 games, damaging his reputation.

Unit R186 — Topic Area 3: Negative Effects of the Media in Sport

Negative Effects of the Media in Sport

Performers' Private Lives can Make the News

1) Details of many sports performers' private lives are often exposed by the media.
2) This can have a negative impact on a performer's mental health and can damage the reputation of many sporting heroes.

EXAMPLES
- In 2016, WADA files were leaked in the media, revealing that British cyclist Sir Bradley Wiggins had taken allergy medication before some of his major wins. He was found innocent of doping, but the media had unfairly questioned his achievements at the Olympic Games and the Tour de France.
- England rugby player Danny Cipriani received negative media coverage in 2018 when he was arrested for assaulting a police officer.
- Naomi Osaka became the first Japanese tennis player to win a major singles title. In 2021, Osaka withdrew from press conferences due to the negative impact on her mental health. She received a mixed reaction for this decision, and sparked many conversations about how mental health is addressed in sport.

Performers, Officials and Coaches Face Criticism

1) The media's analysis of performance and refereeing decisions puts sports performers and officials under a lot of pressure. Key moments are often replayed and debated.
2) Social media means that the general public can also easily voice their opinions online, which can have an impact on the mental health of performers, officials and coaches.

EXAMPLES
- After missing penalties in the UEFA EURO 2020 final, Bukayo Saka, Jadon Sancho and Marcus Rashford all received racial abuse online.
- In 2022, international rugby union referee Wayne Barnes revealed that he almost gave up refereeing because of online criticism and abuse.

Leaving negative comments about someone online is sometimes known as 'trolling'.

The Media Draws Attention to How Performers Look

1) Different sports suit different body types, e.g. high jumpers are much leaner than weightlifters.
2) However, there are instances in the media (e.g. on social media) where language or images are used that promote the idea that everyone should have the same 'ideal' body shape.
3) This is unrealistic, and puts pressure on performers to look a certain way.

EXAMPLES
- Serena Williams experienced body shaming throughout her tennis career because of her muscular build.
- Katelyn Ohashi, a gymnast who went viral in 2019 for her 'perfect 10' routine, spoke about her experience of body shaming after putting on weight after an injury.

Female performers generally have to deal with negative comments about their appearance more often than male performers do.

The secret to doing well in the assessment is [REDACTED]...
Use these pages to inspire your own research. There are lots of examples of performers, teams and events in every sport that have been impacted by media coverage. Spend some time making your own notes.

Unit R186 — Topic Area 3: Negative Effects of the Media in Sport

Provision of Outdoor Activities

Each outdoor activity covered on the next two pages (except camping) is from the OCR approved activity list.

Outdoor Activities are Adventurous

1) Outdoor or adventurous activities are done in natural settings or at specially-built recreation areas.
2) They are a great way of being active and learning new skills.
3) Some activities are challenging and can give you a chance to explore new places.
4) Most outdoor activities have their own National Governing Body (NGB) (see p.32-34) — look at the appropriate NGB website for more information on each activity.

There Are Lots of Different Outdoor Activities

Water Sports

1) **Canoeing** and **kayaking**:
   - Canoeing involves paddling a canoe with a single-bladed paddle.
   - Kayaking is very similar to canoeing, but a double-bladed paddle is used.
   - You can canoe or kayak on lakes, rivers, canals or the sea.
   - British Canoeing is the NGB for both activities.
2) **Sailing** and **windsurfing**:
   - Sailing involves using the wind to move a boat with a sail across water.
   - Windsurfing is similar to sailing, but the sail is attached to a board.
   - You can sail or windsurf on lakes or the sea.
   - Royal Yachting Association is the NGB for both activities.

Brace yourselves, it's a bit choppy ahead.

Many outdoor activities can be done in groups or individually, e.g. you can use a solo canoe or one that seats up to four people.

Trekking

Trekking (or hiking) is walking in a natural environment and on trails.

1) **Hill walking** and **mountaineering**:
   - Hill walking is walking in an upland area, often with the aim of climbing to the top of a hill.
   - Mountaineering is climbing mountains. This often involves scrambling and rock climbing.
   - There are many mountainous and hilly areas in North West England, Wales and Scotland where these activities are possible.
   - The British Mountaineering Council (BMC) is the NGB for hill walking and mountaineering.
2) **Orienteering**:
   - Orienteering is navigating through an unfamiliar, rough area using a map and compass. Participants must find control points (marked checkpoints) along the route.
   - Orienteering can take place anywhere, but often happens in forests and remote areas.
   - British Orienteering is the NGB.

Camping

1) Camping is sleeping in an outdoor area (usually in the countryside) in a tent.
2) **Wild camping**:
   - Wild camping is camping that isn't at a designated campsite.
   - Wild camping is legal in most of Scotland, but it's illegal in the rest of the UK without permission.

Camping isn't on the approved activity list, so you can't choose it for your assessment.

Provision of Outdoor Activities

Climbing

1) Climbing is scaling a mountain or rock face, usually with a rope, harness and belay device.
2) **Single-pitch climbing** is climbing from one pitch (point) to another using one length of rope.
3) **Abseiling** involves descending down a rock face.
4) The British Mountaineering Council (BMC) is the NGB for climbing.

A belay device allows another climber to apply tension to the rope to prevent you from falling very far.

Caving

1) **Caving** (potholing) involves exploring underground caves, usually by crawling and squeezing through narrow spaces.
2) **Mine exploration** is similar, but takes place in abandoned mines or quarries and usually involves less crawling as there is more space.
3) The British Caving Association is the NGB for caving.

Cycling

1) **Mountain biking** is cycling off-road using a mountain bike.
2) **Trail biking** is a form of mountain biking, which involves steep, technical trails.
3) **BMX racing** is also off-road, but involves sprint racing on a single-lap track.
4) British Cycling is the NGB for cycling.

Gliding

1) **Hang gliding** involves flying a small, light aircraft without an engine, which is made of a frame covered in cloth. The pilot is attached by a harness and usually launches themselves from a hill.
2) **Paragliding** is similar to hang gliding, but the pilot is attached to a parachute-like canopy.
3) The British Hang Gliding and Paragliding Association is the NGB for gliding.

Snow Sports

1) **Snowboarding** involves descending a snow-covered surface on a snowboard.
2) **Skiing** is similar, but your feet are attached to skis, rather than a snowboard.
3) **Snowshoeing** involves hiking across snow using snowshoes. These shoes help to spread your weight so you can walk on top of the snow rather than through it.
4) GB Snowsport is the NGB for snow sports.

Other Land-Based Activities

1) **Gorge walking** is scrambling up or down rivers and small waterfalls.
2) **Canyoning** is similar to gorge walking, but involves larger drops — climbing, abseiling and swimming are often required.
3) **Sea level traversing** involves scrambling or climbing along sea cliffs using ropes.
4) **Coasteering** is similar to sea level traversing, but you move along the coastline by swimming or on foot.
5) **High ropes courses** are obstacle courses in treetops with ladders, nets, tightropes and ziplines.

Provision of Outdoor Activities

National Sports Centres Provide Specialist Facilities

National sports centres are large sites that provide specialist facilities, equipment and expertise. Staff are employed to lead training and competitions, and there is usually accommodation available. Here are some examples of national sports centres for outdoor activities:

EXAMPLES

- Holme Pierrepoint in Nottinghamshire is home to the National Water Sports Centre. It features a regatta lake (a wide lake for rowing and sailing) and a white-water slalom course.
- Tollymore National Outdoor Centre is the Northern Ireland Centre for Mountaineering and Canoeing. It's located on the edge of the Mourne Mountains and is funded by Sport Northern Ireland.
- Plas y Brenin in Wales is home to a National Outdoor Centre, funded by Sport England. It offers activities such as hill walking, mountain biking and canoeing.

Voluntary Organisations Support Young People

Voluntary organisations provide opportunities for people under 18 to try outdoor activities. Groups are run by volunteers and aim to help young people develop various skills.

EXAMPLES

- The Scouts encourage children of different ages to take part in activities such as camping, canyoning and coasteering in order to develop skills, e.g. teamwork and commitment.
- Girlguiding is the largest youth organisation for girls in the UK. Its aim is to empower girls through adventurous challenges. It offers a range of outdoor activities including kayaking, hill walking and climbing.
- Cadet organisations, including the Sea Cadet Corps and the Army Cadets, encourage young people to participate in adventure activities such as sailing, canoeing and orienteering to help them develop life skills.
- The Duke of Edinburgh's Award is a youth awards programme with three levels — Bronze, Silver and Gold. Each award has different sections that must be completed, including volunteering, a physical section, a skills section and an expedition.

Local Providers Include Commercial Sports Centres

Local outdoor activity providers are usually private companies with purpose-built activity centres.

EXAMPLES

- Go Ape is an outdoor adventure company with centres all over the UK. They offer high ropes courses, zip lining and off-road trails for personal transporters.
- PGL also has several centres across the UK, which are popular choices for school trips and summer camps. They offer a variety of outdoor activities including climbing, kayaking, sailing, orienteering and high ropes courses.

Did you hear about the monarch on the mountain? He was a hiking...

In the assessment, you'll need to write about the national and local provision of outdoor activities. Try this task — research an activity centre in your local area, and list all of the outdoor activities they provide.

Unit R187 — Topic Area 1: Provision of Outdoor Activities

Equipment, Clothing and Technology

Outdoor activities can be dangerous, so it's important to use the right equipment, clothing and technology.

Different Activities Need Appropriate Equipment and Clothing

Safety Equipment

Equipment that protects from injury:
- A life jacket or buoyancy aid keeps you afloat if you capsize when kayaking.
- A helmet protects your head, and a harness stops you from falling when rock climbing.

Specialist Equipment

Specific equipment needed for an activity:
- A canoe and paddle for canoeing.
- A compass (for navigation) for orienteering.
- A tent, stove and sleeping bag for camping.

Safety Clothing

Clothing that protects from injury:
- Walking boots help support the ankle on rough terrain when hiking.
- Rock shoes support the feet when climbing and provide extra grip.

Specialist Clothing

Specific clothing needed for an activity:
- A wetsuit keeps you warm even if you get wet — useful for water sports.
- Thermal clothing is thin and traps heat. It keeps you warm in cold weather — useful for snow sports.
- Wicking tops help to remove sweat — they keep you dry in intense activities, e.g. BMX racing.

General Clothing

Everyday clothing appropriate for some activities:
- Wellington boots keep your feet dry when gorge walking.
- A hat, gloves and fleece help to keep you warm when hiking.
- Waterproof / windproof jackets and trousers protect against the rain and wind when camping.

Technology Helps Participants in Several Ways

Technology has many useful roles for people participating in outdoor activities.

1. **Access and transportation** — technology helps participants move around more easily. E.g. snow mobiles and quad bikes can transport heavy equipment over rough terrain.
2. **Comfort** — clothing and equipment are made with lighter materials. This makes participants more comfortable and reduces the risk of exhaustion.
3. **Safety** — technology keeps participants safe in unknown terrain. E.g. GPS tracks exact locations, so participants won't get lost. Personal distress beacons can also quickly contact local rescue teams.
4. **Communication** — technology allows for easy communication. E.g. participants can use waterproof walkie talkies to talk to each other, even during water and snow sports.
5. **Information** — technology provides access to a lot of information. E.g. participants can use smartwatches and smartphones to check weather reports before heading out on a hike.

Not quite the rescue service I had in mind...

I'm feeling gorge-ous in my new wellington boots...

Here's some assessment practice for you — choose an outdoor activity and write a list of the equipment, clothing and technology you need to participate, explaining how they help improve participation or safety.

Types of Terrain and Environment

Outdoor activities usually need a specific type of terrain or environment for participation.

Activities Need Specific Types of Terrain

1) Terrain is an area of land that has specific physical features.
2) Each outdoor activity needs a specific terrain or environment — it can be natural or man-made.
3) Some activities also need the right climate, e.g. skiing in a natural environment requires a cold climate.
4) Here are the types of terrain and environment that you need to know:

Terrain/Environment	Description	Example activities
Lake	Body of water surrounded by land.	Canoeing, kayaking, sailing, windsurfing.
Sea	Body of water that covers most of the Earth.	Canoeing, kayaking, sailing, windsurfing, coasteering, sea level traversing.
River	Natural, flowing waterway.	Canoeing, kayaking.
Canal	Man-made waterway.	Canoeing, kayaking.
Forest	Area of wooded land.	Cycling, walking, camping, orienteering, high ropes courses.
Moorland	Area of high, open land that is often boggy.	Cycling, hill walking, wild camping, orienteering.
Quarry	An open pit where materials are mined.	Mine exploration, caving, climbing, abseiling.
Crag	Steep cliff or rock face.	Climbing, abseiling, sea level traversing.
Gorge	Narrow, steep-walled passage with a stream.	Canyoning, gorge walking.
Mountainous area	Area with mountains and steep ground.	Mountaineering, hill walking, climbing, camping, mountain biking, snowshoeing.
Indoor ski slope	Man-made indoor venue with slopes made of real snow.	Snowboarding, skiing.
Dry ski slope	Man-made outdoor venue with slopes made of plastic that mimics real snow.	Snowboarding, skiing.

National Parks

1) National parks are protected areas of countryside — there are 15 national parks in the UK.
2) Examples include the Lake District, Dartmoor and the Pembrokeshire Coast.
3) They often have a variety of terrains, such as lakes, gorges, crags and forests.
4) Water sports, climbing, hiking, cycling, caving and high ropes courses are all popular outdoor activities in the national parks.

Natural areas, like forests and national parks, often include trails (walking or cycling paths).

What an interesting terrain of thought...

The need for specific terrains and environments mean that people usually have to travel to participate in outdoor activities. Research the terrains in your local area or region and the activities that are possible.

Unit R187 — Topic Area 2: Equipment, Clothing and Safety